A CORNISH SMUGGLER

PRINTED BY

SPOTTISWOODE AND CO., NEW-STREET SQUARE

LONDON

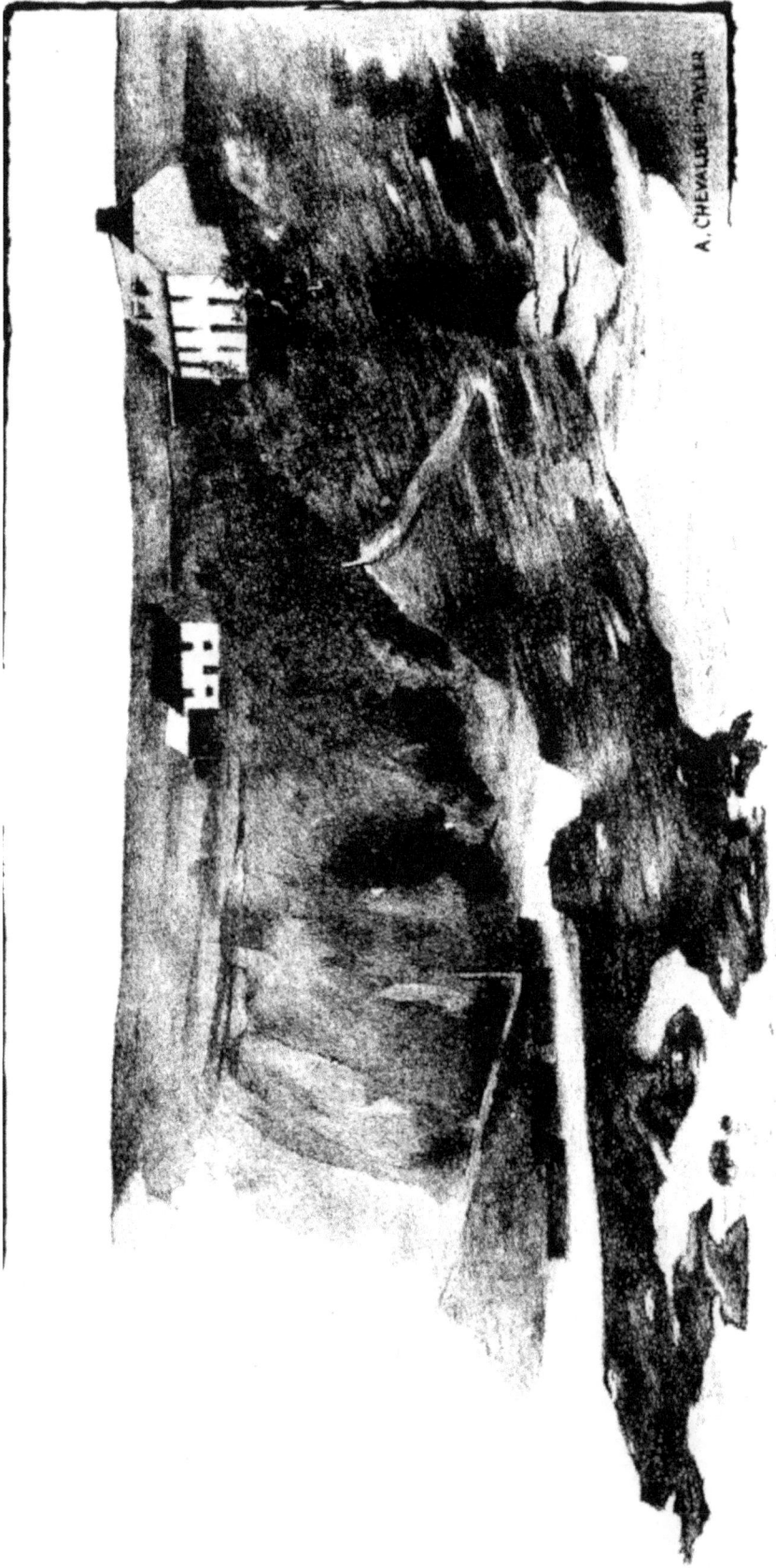

A. CHEVALIER-TAYLER

BESSIE'S COVE FROM THE ENEZ POINT.

THE AUTOBIOGRAPHY

OF A

CORNISH SMUGGLER

(CAPTAIN HARRY CARTER, OF PRUSSIA COVE)

1749–1809

WITH AN INTRODUCTION AND NOTES
BY
JOHN B. CORNISH

Truro
JOSEPH POLLARD, 5 ST. NICHOLAS STREET
LONDON: GIBBINGS & CO., 18 BURY STREET, W.C.
1894

INTRODUCTION

THE existence of the Autobiography which is published in the following pages came to my knowledge in the course of a chance conversation with a distant relative of the writer's family. The original manuscript has been carefully preserved, and has been for many years in the possession of Mr. G. H. Carter, of Helston. He received it from his father, the G. Carter mentioned on page 1, who was a nephew of Harry Carter himself. The memoir of the writer, which will be found in the 'Wesleyan Methodist Magazine' for October 1831, was based upon information supplied by G. Carter partly from the manuscript and partly from his own knowledge. The original is now printed in full for the first time, with the consent of the family.

The part of Cornwall to which the autobiography chiefly relates is the district lying between the two small towns of Marazion and Helston, a distance of about ten miles on the north-eastern shores of Mounts

Bay, comprising the parishes of Breage, Germoe, St. Hilary, and Perranuthnoe. The bay is practically divided into two parts by Cuddan Point, a sharp small headland about two miles east from St. Michael's Mount. The western part runs into the land in a roughly semicircular shape, and is so well sheltered that it has almost the appearance of a lake, and, in fact, the extreme north-western corner is called Gwavas Lake. From the hills which surround it the land everywhere slopes gently to the sea, and is thickly inhabited. The towns of Penzance and Marazion and the important fishing village of Newlyn occupy a large portion of the shore, and around them are woody valleys and well cultivated fields. To the eastward of Cuddan is a marked contrast. There, steep and rocky cliffs are only broken by two long stretches of beach, Pra Sand and the Looe Bar, on which the great seas which come always from the Atlantic make landing impossible except on a few rare summer days. With the exception of the little fishing station of Porthleven there is not a place all along the coast, from Cuddan Point to the Lizard, large enough to be called a village. Inland the country is in keeping with the character of the coast. Trees are very scarce, and the stone hedges, so characteristic of all the wild parts of West Cornwall, the patches of moorland, and the scattered cottages make the whole appearance bare and exposed.

Porth Leah, or the King's Cove, now more usually

known as Prussia Cove,[1] around which so much of the interest of the narrative centres, lies a little to the eastward of Cuddan Point. There are really two coves divided from one another by a point and a small island called the 'Enez.' The western cove, generally called 'Bessie's Cove,' is a most sheltered and secluded place. It is so well hidden from the land that it is impossible to see what boats are lying in the little harbour until one comes down to the very edge of the cliff. The eastern side of the point, where there is another small harbour, called the 'King's Cove,' is more open, but the whole place is thoroughly out of the world even now.

The high road from Helston through Marazion to Penzance now passes about a mile from the sea, but at the time of which Harry Carter was writing this district must have been unknown and almost inaccessible. From all accounts West Cornwall at that time was very little more than half civilised. The mother of Sir Humphry Davy (born at Penzance, 1778) has left us a record that when she was a girl 'West Cornwall was without roads,

---

[1] It is said that this name is derived from the fact that John Carter, a brother of Harry Carter, and the most famous of the smugglers, lived there. He was nicknamed the 'King of Prussia,' and the house in which he lived is still known as the 'King of Prussia's House.' The origin of this nickname is explained by a story that when they were all boys together, they used to play at soldiers, and John would always claim to be the King of Prussia. Clearly an echo of the fame of Frederick the Great had reached these boys about the time of the Seven Years' War.

there was only one cart in the town of Penzance, and packhorses were in use in all the country districts' (Bottrell, iii. 150). This is confirmed by a writer in the 'Gentleman's Magazine,' who says that in 1754 there were no roads in this district, the ways that served the purpose were merely bridle paths 'remaining as the deluge left them and dangerous to travel over' ('Gent. Mag.,' Oct. 1754); and by the official records of the town of Penzance, which show that in 1760 the Corporation went to some expense in opposing the extension of the turnpike beyond Marazion, to which place it was then first carried from Penryn (Millett's 'Penzance, Past and Present').

The places of which the names are mentioned in the autobiography, but which are not shown in the map, such as Rudgeon, Trevean, Caerlean, Pengersick, Kenneggey, and Rinsey, are all in the immediate neighbourhood of Prussia Cove. They are merely little hamlets of four or five cottages each, and there is no reason to suppose that they were any larger one hundred years ago. Helston, the market town of the district, is about six miles off, and had then a population of some two thousand people.

The chief interest in the autobiography is probably that which it attracts as the most authentic account of the smuggling which was carried on in the neighbourhood in the latter portion of the last century. Cornwall has long enjoyed a certain reputation for pre-eminence in this particular form of trade, and apparently not without some reason. A series of letters of the years 1750—1753 were published some years ago in the journal of the Royal Institution of Cornwall (vol. vi. pt. xxii. p. 374, 'The Lanisley Letters') to a Lieutenant-General Onslow, from George Borlase, his agent at Penzance, asking that soldiers might be stationed in the district, because 'the coasts here swarm with smugglers,' and mentioning that a detachment ought to be stationed at Helston, as 'just on that neighborhood lye the smugglers and wreckers more than about us, tho' there are too many in all parts of this country.' In his 'Natural History of Cornwall,' published in 1758, Dr. Borlase regrets (p. 312) that 'the people of the sea coast are, it must be owned, too much addicted to carry off our bullion to France and to bring back nothing but brandy, tea, and other luxuries.' This is delicate, but there can be no doubt of his meaning; and he goes on to complain that 'there is not the poorest family in any parish which has not its tea, its snuff, and tobacco, and (when they have money or credit) brandy,' all, we may presume, duty free. The will of Philip Hawkins, M.P. for Grampound, who died on September 6, 1738, is perhaps the most striking record, for he actually bequeathed 600*l*. to the king to compensate for the amount to which his tenants had defrauded the Customs.

That the smuggling prevailed to such an extent is not to be wondered at, for the law must have had but a very slight hold on such a rough and scattered population, living so far away from any of the large centres of England. In such a narrow country too, where no one lives very far from the sea, the miners took to smuggling as readily as the fishermen. A trip to Roscoff or Guernsey formed a pleasant change after a spell on tribute underground or working stamps. A rough, reckless, and drunken lot were these tinners, and if riots and bloodshed were more scarce in West Cornwall than in some parts, it must have been due to the judicious absence of the Custom House officials, and not to any qualities in the smugglers. George Borlase says ('Lanisley Letters') that in December 1750 a Dutch ship laden with claret was wrecked near Helston, and 'in twenty-four hours the tinners cleared all,' the authorities apparently not daring to interfere; and that just before a man who went to the assistance of the revenue officers had been killed near the same place.

Beyond these I have mentioned, the literary records are very meagre, but the whole county, and especially the western part, abounds with legends. The smuggling was so universal, that every cove and fishing village on the coast has its own stories, and everywhere the curious visitor is still shown the place where the smugglers landed their cargoes, the secret caves where they stored them, and sometimes, but not often, the places where the 'officers' found them. Prussia Cove, beyond all others, has the richest store of such history. Here are little harbours cut out of the solid rock, which are now occupied by innocent fishing boats. The visitor can see a roadway, partly cut and partly worn, crossing the rocks below high water mark, and caves of which the mouths have been built up, and which are reputed to be connected with the house on the cliff above by secret passages.

In the legends of the Cove the personality of John Carter looms so large that his associates are almost if not entirely forgotten, and everything centres around him alone. It was he who cut the harbours and the road, it was he who adapted the caves, and he is the hero of most of the tales which are told of the good old days. One of these stories is worth recording. On one occasion, during his absence from home, the excise officers from Penzance came around in their boats and took a cargo, which had lately arrived from France, to Penzance, where it was secured in the Custom House store. In due course John Carter returned to the Cove and learned the news. What was he to do? He explained to his comrades that he had agreed to deliver that cargo to the customers by a certain day, and his reputation as an honest man was at stake. He must keep his word. That night a number of armed men broke open the stores at Penzance, and the ' King of Prussia ' took his own again, returning to the Cove without being discovered. In the morning the officers found that the place had been broken open during the night.

They examined the contents, and when they noted what particular things were gone, they said to one another that John Carter had been there, and they knew it, because he was an honest man who would not take anything that did not belong to him. And John Carter kept his word to his customers. The story that he once opened fire on a revenue cutter from a small battery which he had made at the Cove is well known along the coast.

It is characteristic of the history of the smugglers everywhere that they enjoyed the support of popular sympathy. This was certainly the case in West Cornwall, where the farmers, the merchants, and, it is rumoured, the local magistrates, used to find the money with which the business was carried on, investing small sums in each voyage. Harry Carter finding shelter at Marazion when the Government were offering a reward for his capture (p. 19), and the action of the unnamed 'great man of the neighbourhood' on his return from America (p. 63), are perhaps the reverse of the picture which George Borlase drew for General Onslow ('Lanisley Letters'); 'the countenance given to the smugglers by those whose business it is to restrain these pernicious practices, hath bro't 'em so bold and daring that nobody can venture to come near them with safety whilst they are at their work.' It is difficult to avoid the conclusion that there must have been some powerful influence exerted in his favour to obtain his exchange from prison in France in 1778, and what else can we make of the commission to go privateering against the Americans. The Government had then recently passed a measure[1] to encourage privateering by authorising the Admiralty to grant commissions, and apparently English sailors were everywhere readily taking advantage of the opportunity so afforded for their enterprise.[2] But to obtain such a commission the applicant had to find the security of sureties, of whose 'sufficiency' the commissioners were to satisfy themselves, and also to send in a written application specifying the ship for which the commission was asked, with full details as to the number of her guns and other matters. He surely could not have ventured to place himself in the hands of the Government in this way without a friend at Court. It certainly seems a fair inference from their popularity, their fame, and from the fact that they both rose to leading positions amongst the smugglers while still comparatively young, that Harry Carter and his brother John were superior men to the rough material of which their crews were probably composed.

The accounts of the actual smuggling in the following pages are not very elaborate, but we must remember that at the time when Harry Carter was writing (1809), John Carter and the 'Cove boys' were

---

[1] 17 Geo. III. c. 7.
[2] See Lecky. *History of Eighteenth Century*, vol. iv. ch. xiv.

still at it, and Prussia Cove had not yet ceased to be a great centre of smugglers. This would also explain the absence of any more particular reference to any of his companions. This reticence, which we must respect, although we may regret it, is quite compensated for by the variety of his later experiences. To have been a prisoner in France during the Reign of Terror, and at a time when the Convention had decreed that no quarter should be given to an Englishman,[1] is of itself no small claim on the attention of his countrymen. From his account, which is, I believe, unique in English literature, and especially when it is compared with those of French writers, it would seem that the English, who were, of course, prisoners of war, were placed on the same footing as the 'aristocrats' and 'suspects,' the great number of whom made it necessary to utilise the convents and even private houses as prisons. Alexandrine des Echerolles tells us ('Private Life in Public Calamities') that 'Bread was distributed daily to the prisoners, and their pitchers were filled every morning with fresh water. Those who could not pay the turnkeys for their trouble got none, so the rich used to bestow alms upon the poor in this form. . . . Once a fortnight, I think, they were supplied with fresh straw, or what was called such, each person received an armful.' She mentions that by degrees the prisoners managed to make themselves more comfortable by introducing

---

[1] Carlyle. *French Revolution,* bk. iii. ch. iv.

tables, and chairs, and mattresses, which they were compelled to leave behind on their removal to other prisons. All this coincides very closely with Harry Carter's account, and he seems to have shared their anxiety as to the fate of his friends and the common anticipation of the guillotine.

Even this does not exhaust the interest of his life. The very first lines of his writing show the object with which he wrote. In no part of England did the teaching and influence of John Wesley obtain such a hold as in Cornwall. At the time of his first visit he speaks of the natives of this distant country as 'those who neither feared God nor regarded man' ('Diary,' May 17, 1743); he accuses them of wrecking and of murdering those who were washed ashore, and describes their pastimes as 'hurling, at which limbs were often broken, fighting, drinking, and all other manner of wickedness.' The 'Lanisley Letters' contain similar charges of wrecking and murder, and Dr. Borlase confirms the statement as to their drunken habits. In 1750 Wesley mentions how greatly all these things were changed. They were, perhaps, not as much changed as he thought, but undoubtedly they were greatly improved, for it is plain fact that the whole of the moral reformation of the Cornish folk is due to him. He gained followers so rapidly in the west that at the first Methodist Conference in 1744, St. Ives is classed with London, Bristol, and Newcastle; 'from this it is evident,' says Dr. Smith

('Hist. of Methodism,' i. 213), 'that London, Bristol, St. Ives, and Newcastle were regarded as the great centres of Methodism in England at this period.' At the third Conference (1746) Cornwall forms one district out of seven, while the others included in some cases four and in one case six English counties. In 1750 John Wesley ('Diary,' August 18) says of St. Just, 'There is still the largest society in Cornwall, and so great a proportion of believers I have not found in all the nation beside.' Similar societies or classes sprang up in the most remote places, such as Rugan, or Rudgeon as it is more usually spelt now, where the society met at which Charles Carter was converted; at Trevean and Caerlean, where Harry Carter preached.

That especial characteristic of Wesley's organisation, 'the local preacher,' took root firmly in Cornwall from the very first. To those who are not acquainted with the county it may be necessary to explain that these laymen, earnest men of all classes, who preach, are so common in every village that they constitute a distinguishing feature in the local life. The services in the small wayside chapels which are so numerous are usually conducted by a local preacher in the intervals between the visits of the regular ministers. Those who do know Cornwall also know the importance of the local preacher in the history of the Methodist movement. John Wesley's preaching was received by the poor and uneducated, the miner, the fisherman, and the labourer, and the persecution of the clergy and the magistrates only strengthened the enthusiasm of the people for their great teacher. From such men sprang the first local preachers ; preaching and exhorting not with the dull formality of men who had to do it, but with the earnestness of men who really felt that they had a message to deliver, and labouring under uncontrollable excitement they greatly impressed their hearers ; while the familiarity of their persons led their audience to look upon this new teaching as a thing of their own to which they could all attain. It is impossible to doubt that the hold which the movement gained was greatly due to these men, and Harry Carter was one of them. John Wesley had set himself from the first against the smuggling which he found so prevalent ; he had preached against it at several places, and had even published a pamphlet against it. We may therefore fairly suppose that Harry Carter, the great smuggler, was regarded as a most important accession to the ranks of his followers.

The autobiography ends abruptly in the year 1795, but the writer lived until April 19, 1829. The last thirty years of his life he spent at Rinsey. He lived quietly, keeping himself occupied with a small farm, and occasionally preaching in the neighbourhood. From the memoir of him in the 'Wesleyan Methodist Magazine,' to which I have already referred, I cull the two further facts that he retained the intensity of his religious feelings up to his death, and that he never failed in grateful recollections of James Macculloch—the Mr. M. of his French prison experiences. Of his family I can learn but little. It is said that originally they came from Shropshire, and certainly the name does not show a Cornish origin. His father, who was called Francis, was born in 1712, and died on February 28, 1774; his mother, Agnes, was born in 1714, and died in 1784. Of the eight sons and two daughters of whom he speaks, I can only trace four of the sons besides himself. Thomas, whom he does not mention, was born in 1737, and died in 1818; and John, whom he refers to as the eldest, Francis, born in 1745, and Charles, born in 1757, and died in 1803, are all mentioned in the autobiography. His daughter, Elizabeth, as far as I can learn, died while young.

In preparing the manuscript for publication I have taken the liberty of omitting some passages here and there which were simply repetitions, and which did not throw any additional light either on the narrative or his character. I have corrected all the wrong spellings which could be classed as simple mistakes, but I have carefully preserved all spellings which appeared of interest, as showing the pronunciation of the words, and especially those which illustrate the local dialect. For instance, the general preference for 'a' over the other vowels, and especially in final syllables, is distinctly characteristic of West Corn-wall.

In some places, particularly towards the end, the manuscript is somewhat damaged, and many of the pages have lost a portion of the lower corner. The gaps so caused I have endeavoured to fill with the words which he probably used, and such words are printed in italics. Where I have been unable to suggest the missing words, I have left blanks.

JOHN B. CORNISH.

PENZANCE, 1894.

ENGLISH CHANNEL

CORNWALL

DEVON

BRITTANY

USHANT

GUERNSEY

ALDERNEY

JERSEY

St Ives

Mount's Bay

The Lizard

Plymouth

The Start

Ushant

Brest

Landernau

I de Bas

St Pol de

Roscoff

Morlaix

Carhaix

Josselin

Dinan

St Malo

C. de la Hague

AUTOBIOGRAPHY

OF

A CORNISH SMUGGLER

———•◇•———

As it have been imprest upon my mind for sevral years to take a memorandum of the kind dealings of God to my soul, in particular these laste two or three years, I have been persuaded by sevral of my friends, in particular Mr. Wormsley and Geo. Carter. I have thought in general it would be so weak that no person of sense would ever publish it to the world, notwithstanding, this morning being 20 of Dec^{r·} 1809, I have taken up my pen, and may the Lord bring past things to my remembrance just[1] as they are, and if published to the world, may the Lord make it a blessing to every soul that read and hear it for Christ's sake, amen, amen.

I have made sevral remarks at difrante times in

---

[1] Spelt 'yest' in the manuscript throughout.

B

years past of sume particular things of my experience for my own amusement, then thinking for no person ever to see it but myself only; and as I have made a general rule more or less for sevral years to have had fixed times to sit in silence to trace my whole life from 8 or 9 years of age, in particular more so since, I have tasted the goodness of God, moste particular things that *I have* past through seems to be tolerable famil*iar* to me.

I was born in the year of 1749 in Pengersick, in the parish of Breage, in the County of Cornwall. My mother had ten children, eight sons and two daghturs, eight of whom lived to maturity. My father was a miner—likewayse rented a little farm of about 12*l.* p^r year—who was a hard labring man, and brought up his family in what we caled [1] decent poverty. My oldest and youngest brothers were brought up to good country scolars, but the rest of my brothers with myself, as soon as we was able, obliged to work in order to contribute a little to help to support a large family, so that I never was keept to scool but only to read in what we caled then the great Book. As for our Religion, we were brought up like the rest of our neighbours, to say some prayers after we were in the bed, and to go to Church on particular times as occasion sarv'd us. When I was aboute 8 or 9 years old, my brother Francis was aboute four years older than me. He joined the methodist society in

---

[1] 'Called.' The spelling is the dialect pronunciation.

Rudgeon,[1] soon after found peace with God, and as him and me was moste times sleeping and waking together he revealed himself unto me, told me the place and time he received the Comfarter. I seeing such very great chainge upon him, as before time he was a very active boy, I farmley believed the report. From that time I farmley believed that except I was born again I should in no case see the kingdom of God, so that convictions followed me sharp and often, sumetimes constrained to weep bitterly. But alas! as I grew up they went fewer[2] and fainter. Aboute 9 or 10 years old went to work to stamps, and continued there until 15 or 16. I worked to bal,[3] as I think, until I was aboute 17, and from thence went with my two oldest brothers to Porthleah[4] or the King's Cove afishing and smuggling, and I think aboute 18 or 19 went at times, with Folston[5] people and sume-times with Irish, as supercargo, whom we freighted. Before this time I larned to write, and so far so, that I would keep my own accounts.

I think I might have been aboute 25 when I went in a small sloop, about 16 or 18[6] tons, with

---

[1] A small village about half a mile from Prussia Cove.

[2] Spelt 'fever' in the manuscript. The Cornish people do not distinguish 'v' and 'w.'

[3] 'Bal' is a mine, tin or copper.

[4] This name is now lost.   [5] ? Folkestone, see p. 56.

[6] The sizes of all his vessels are given in old measurement. Before 1835 ships were measured by the following elaborate rule. Subtract three-fifths of the greatest breadth from the length of the keel, multiply this by the breadth, and the result by half of the breadth; divide the

two men beside myself, asmuggling, where I had very
great success; and after a while I had a new sloop
built for me, about 32 tons.[1]   My success was
rather beyond common, and after a time we bought
a small cuttar of aboute 50 tons[2] and aboute ten
men.   I saild in her one year, and I suppose made
more safe voyages then have been ever made since or
before with any single person.   So by this time I
begun to think some thing of myself, convictions
still following sharply at times.   I allwayse had a dislike to swearing, and made a law on board, if any of
the sailors should swear, was poneshed.   Nevertheless my intention was not pure ; I had sume byends
in it, the bottom of it was only pride, etc.   I wanted to
be noted to be sumething out of the common way of
others, still I allwayse had a dislike to hear others
swearing.   Well, then, I think I was counted what the
world cales a good sort of man, good humoured, not
proude, etc.   But man is short sighted, who can disarn
spirets when the heart is deceitful above all thing and
desparately wicked, oftentimes burning and boiling
within in a blaze of passion, though not to be seen
without.   Nevertheless in the meantime was capable

result so obtained by 94, and the answer is the size of the ship in tons
(see 13 Geo. III. c. 26, § 74).   They are now measured by the cubical
contents.   It is difficult to render these figures in modern measurement, but this sloop was probably about the size which would now be
called 10 tons.

[1] About 18 tons in modern measurement.

[2] About 30 tons in modern measurement.

to be guilty of outward sins the same as others of my companions, and often[1] times, when went out on a party, crying and praying to keep me from a particular sin, was often the first that was guilty of committing it. Then conchance,[2] after staring me in the face, oh what a torment within I felt.[3] So I went on for many years sinning and repenting.

Well, then, in the cource of these few years, as we card[4] a large trade with other vessels allso, we gained a large sum of money, and being a speculating family was not satisfied with small things. Built a new cuttar, aboute 197[5] tons, then one of the first in England ; expecting to make all our fortunes in a hurry. I was in her at sea in Dec.[r] 1777, made one voyage about Christmas. Returning to Guarnsey light, sprung the bowspreat ; was recommended from Guarnsey to St. Malos for a bowspreat, and for the want of Customhouse papars and proper despatchis was seized upon by the admiralty of the above place, where they unbent the sails, took them onshore, and confined us all on board with a gard of soldars as presoners, allowing two men to be on deck only at a time ; likenwayse their orders was for no person to come alongside, no letters to pass or repass. But the comanding officer I soon got in his favour, that I

---

[1] Spelt ' oughten ' in the manuscript. ' Daughter ' is still pronounced ' dafter ' in West Cornwall.

[2] ' Conscience.'   [3] ' Felt,' dialect pronunciation.

[4] ' Carried,' dialect pronunciation.

[5] About 60 tons in modern measurement.

conveyed letters onshore, and sent an express to
Guernsey, likewayse to Roscoff, when there was soon
certificates sent them to certify what I was, as
they stopped me under the pretence of being a
pirate ; their pretence nevertheless was not altogether
unreasonable, I having sixteen carriage guns on
board and thirty-six men without any maritime pass,
or anything to show for them.   Notwithstanding
they certainly knew what I was.   I think it was on
the 30 Jan. 1778, and I think the latter end of
March[1] there was an embargo laid on all English
bottams.   They keept me onboard with all the people
until I think the 1 May, when they took me onshore
in order to examine me, and about four o'clock sent
with a strong gard unto the Castle.   This was a
strange seeing unto me, the first prison I ever saw the
inside of, the hearing of so many iron doors opening,
etc.   So I was put up to the last floor in the top of
that very high Castle, in a criminal jail, where there
were a little short dirty straw, etc.   So after looking
round a little to see my new habitation, I asked of the
jailor to send me a chair to sit on, and sumething to
eat, as I took nothing for the day, then seeming to be
in tolarable spirits ; but as the jailor left me, hearing
the rattling of the doors and the noise of the keys, I
begun to reflect, where am I now ?   I shall shorley
never come out of this place whilst the war lasts,

---

[1] The treaty between France and the Americans was made on
February 6, 1778.

shorley I shall die here, etc. I suppose in the course
of an half hour heard the doors and keys as before
for a long time before I saw any person, so in came a
man with a chair, my bed, and a little soup, etc. Well,
then, I sat myself down in the chair, looked at my
dinner, etc., but then begun to weep bitterly. I had
not loste only my liberty but the cuttar also, which
was my God. My liberty was gone, my honour, my
property, my life, and my God, all was gone ; and all
the ten thousand pounds I expected to get privateering was gone, as there was a commission sent for me
against the Americans before I left home. There I
walked the dismal place bewailing my sad case. But in
the space of aboute two hours two or three of my people
were sent to join me, and before night I think about
eighteen of us, small room full. Then we begun to sing
and make a noise, so that sume of my tears vanished
away ; hope of life sprung up, and as, the Franch was
such flatterers in general, a very little hope for the
cuttar, etc. The remainder of the ship's company put
in the town criminal jail. We was all keept in prison
until aboute the 20 or 21 day of the same month,
when early in the morning were took out by a strong
gard of soldars, sent to Dinan prison of war, where
we had then plenty of room, etc. I suppose we
were aboute six or seven of us that every evening
joined to sing psalms in parts, etc. But this would
not satisfy me, I know there was no Religion in this
at all, but one night as I was asleep, as we lay on

the floor side by side, I dreamed that I heard like the voice of an angel saying unto me, 'Except thou reform thy life, thou must totally be lost for ever.' There was something more that he said, but I cannot now remember it. When I awaked I was in a lake, sweat from head to foot, and all my body in a tremble. Nothing but fear and horror upon my mind. The next day I passed much to myself, very serious and sad, not one smile on my countenance, but keept[1] it all to myself. Took great care to lett no person know anything of the mattar. Well, then, as Cain went to build a city in order to divert his mind, I begun to larn navigation, and so loosed my convictions little and little, that in the course of aboute a fortnight I could do the same as I formely uste to do. I think I was in prison aboute five or six weeks until my oldest brother John[2] was brought to join me, as he come to St. Malas just after I was stopped, from Guarnsey, with certificates from the Governor, etc., in order to try to liberate the cuttar and me. Well, then, this allmoste so great tryal as any, he being the head of the family, and thought the business muste come to an end at home. We was keept both in preson until, as I think, sume time in August, and was sent on parol about forty miles in a town called Josselin. However, we was keeped in difrante places in the country until I think the latter end of Nov[r] in 1779, when we were private ex-

---

[1] 'Kept,' dialect pronunciation. 　　　[2] The 'King of Prussia.'

changed, by the order of the Lords of the Admiralty, in the room of two French gentlemen sent to France in our room. And then to come by the way of Ostend, being, as well I can remember, aboute five hundred miles. From thence came by the way of London, and arived at home the 24 Decr. in the same year. We found the family all alive and well, but with the loss of the cuttar, and the business not managed well at home, as my brother was then a presoner, and wanting from home aboute two years, the family in a low state. Nevertheless, he being well respected with the Guarnsey marchants, was offered credit with many of them. So went on again in freighting of large vessels, and had very good speed for sume time. I went again in the little cuttar I had before, aboute 50 tons.[1] And after making two or three voyages to the King's Cove, went with a cargo on the coast of Wales. In order to smuggle it, went onshore to sell it. Left the cuttar to anchor near the Mumbles, where an information was given to an armship called the ' Three Brothers,' that lay sume distance from there. And aboute that time there had been some large privateers' cuttars on that coast from Dunkirk, and had taken may prizes, manned and commanded chiefly with Irishmen. My cuttar was represented to be one of them, namely, the ' Black Prince,' mounting sixteen guns and sixty men. I had then

---

[1] Cf. note 6, p. 3.

in the cuttar about six men and three beside myself onshore. When they saw the armship coming upon them, cut the cable and went to sea; and when the ship gave up the chase from the cuttar, sent his boats onshore, took up the cuttar's cable and anchor, and found me onshore. I having left my commission on board, and had nothing to show who or what I was, took me on board the ship as a pirate, and after examining me in the cabin for two or three hours, detained me as a prisoner for twelve weeks until I was cleared by my friends at home through the Lords of the Admiralty. So after I was at home some time, riding about the country getting freights, collecting money for the company, etc. etc., we bought a cuttar aboute 160 tons,[1] nineteen guns. I went in her sumetime asmuggling, and had great success. We had a new luggar built, which mounted twenty guns, and both went in company together from Guarnsey, smuggling along the coast, so that by this time I begun to think sumething of myself again. Nevertheless convictions never left me long together. But in the course of this time, being exposed to more company and sailors of all descriptions, larned to swear at times. And once, after discharging our cargo, brought the both vessels to an anchor in Newlyn[2] Road, when we had an express sent us from St. Ives of a large cuttar

[1] About 50 tons in modern measurement.
[2] Newlyn, near Penzance.

privateer from Dunkirk, called the 'Black Prince,' had been on that coast and had taken many prizes, to go out in pursuit of her. It was not a very agreeable business, notwithstanding for fear to offend the collector,[1] we put round the both vessels to St. Ives Roade, and after staying there two or three days, the same cuttar hove in sight Christmas day in the morning. We not having our proper crews on board, colected a few[2] men together, and went to sea in pursuit of him. Soon come up with him, so that after a running fight for three or four hours, as we, not being half manned, and the sea very big, the shots so uncertain, the luggar received a shot that was obliged to bear up, and in the course of less then an hour after I received a shot that card of my jib, and another in the hull, that we could hardly keep her free. So that we bore up after the luggar, not knowing what was the matter of her running away. We came up with her aboute five in the evning. Desired the Captain to quitt her, but he, in hope to put her into Padstow, continued pumping and bailing until aboute six, when he hail'd me, saying, stand by him, he was going to quitt her. So that they hoisted out their boate, but the sea being so bigg and the men being confused, filled her with water, so that they could not free her nomore. I got my boat out in the meantime, sent her alongside the luggar, so

[1] The collector of the Customs, presumably at Penzance.
[2] Spelt 'feve' in the manuscript. Cf. note 2, p. 3.

that some of the men jumpt over board, and my boate pickt them up, and immediately the luggar went down. I hove to the cuttar and laid her to, that she drifted right over the place that the luggar went down, so that some of the men got on board by virtue of ropes hove from the cuttar, sume got hold of the jib tack, and sume pickt up by the cuttar's boate, so that we saved alive seventeen men and fourteen drowned. As Providence would have it was aboute the full of the moon, or certainly all must be lost. This was scene indeed. What cries! what screeches! what confusion was there! We stayed some little time there cruising aboute the place, but soon obliged to get the cuttar under a double reefed trysail, a heavy gale of wind ensuing, and bore up for the Mumbles. Now I am going to inform you of a little more of my pride and vanity, the spirit of truth had not as yet forgot to strive with me. Before we come up with the privateer, in expecting to come to an engagement, oh, what horror was upon my mind for fear of death, as I know I must come to judgment sure and sartin. If I died, I should be lost for ever. Notwithstanding all this I made the greatest outward show of bravery, and, through pride and presumption, exposed myself to the greatest danger. I stood on the companion until the wad of the enemies' shot flew in fire aboute me, and I suppose the wind of the shot struck me down on the deck as the shot took in the mainsail right in a line with me. One of my officers helpt me up, thought I was wounded, and he would not suffer me to go there nomore. This was a great salvation, and that of God, and not the only one ; for all so many hundreds of shot have flyed around me, I never received somuch as a blemish in one of my fingers ; but I can remember for many years before this, whenever I expected to come to an engagement, I was allwayse struck with horror of mind, knowing I was not fit to die ; and since I have tasted of the goodness of God, I have thought that the greatest hero in the Army or Navy, as long as the spirit of Truth continue to strive with them, even Anson, is struck with the like feelings ; and if ever I hear of a coward, I know this is the cause of it.

In the year of 19th April, 1786, I was married to Elizabeth Flindel, of Helford, in the parish of Manaccan, and in April 19, in 1787, she bore me a daughter, who was called after her mother's name, and I think it was aboute midle of Nov[r.] I went in a luggar, asmuggling, about 140[1] tons, mounting sixteen carriage guns. After making one voyage at home to the King's Cove I got a freight for Costan,[2] and as I depended on them people to look out if there were any danger, according to their promise, came into the Bay, and after sume time spoke with a boate from the above place, saying it was a clear coast, there was no danger to bring the vessel up to anchor, and we should have boats enough

---

[1] About 45 tons in modern measurement.
[2] ? Cawsand, near Plymouth.

out to discharge all the cargo immediately.   So that I brought the vessel to anchor, leaving the jib with the trysail and mizen set, and begun to make ready, opening the hatches, etc., when I saw two boats rowing up from the shore.   I said to the pilot, 'There is two boats acoming.' He answered, 'They are our boats coming to take the goods out,' etc. Soon after a boat come alongside. 'Do you know these is two man-o'-war's boats ?' We immediately cutt the cable, and before the luggar gathered headway were right under the starn.   They immediately cutt off the mizen sheet, and with a musket shot shot off the trysal tack and boarded us over the starn.   My people having sume muskets, dropt them down and went below.   I knowing nothing of that, thought that all would stand by me.   I begun to engage them as well as I could without anything in my hands, as they took us in surprise so suddenly, I having my great coat on buttoned aboute me, I seeing none of my people, only one man at the helm ; and when they saw no person to oppose them, turned upon me with their broad swords, and begun to beat away upon my head.   I found the blows very heavey—crushed me down to the deck—and as I never loosed my senses, rambled forward.   They still pursued me, beating and pushing me, so that I fell down on the deck on a small raft just out of their way.   I suppose I might have been there aboute a quarter of an hour, until they had secured my people below, and after found me laying on the deck.   One of them said, ' Here is one of the poor fellows dead.' Another made answer, ' Put the man below.' He answered again, saying, ' What use is it to put a dead man below ?' and so past on. Aboute this time the vessel struck aground, the wind being about East S.E. very hard, right on the shore. So there I laid very quiet for near the space of two hours, hearing their discourse as they walked by me, the night being very dark on the 30 Jan^y· 1788. When some of them saw me lying there, said, ' Here lays one of the fellows dead,' one of them answered as before, ' Put him below.' Another said, ' The man is dead.' The commanding officer gave orders for a lantern and candle to be brought, so they took up one of my legs, as I was lying upon my belly ; he let it go, and it fell as dead down on the deck. He likewayse put his hand up under my clothes, between my shirt and my skin, and then examined my head, and so concluded, saying, ' The man is so warm now as he was two hours back, but his head is all to atoms.' I have thought hundreds of times since what a miracle it was I neither sneezed, coughed, nor drew breath that they perceived in all this time, I suppose not less than ten or fifteen minutes. The water being ebbing, the vessel making a great heel towards the shore, so that in the course of a very little time after, as their two boats was made fast alongside, one of them broke adrift. Immediately there was orders given to man the other boat in order to fetch her ; so that when I saw them in the state of confusion, their gard broken, I thought it was my time to make my escape, so I crept on my belly on the deck, and got over a large raft just before the main mast, close by one of the men's heels, as he was standing there handing the trysàil. When I got over the lee-side I thought I should be able to swim on shore in a stroke or two. I took hold of the burtins [1] of the mast, and as I was lifting myself over the side, I was taken with the cramp in one of my thighs. So then I thought I should be drowned, but still willing to risk it, so that I let myself over the side very easily by a rope into the water, fearing my enemies would hear me and then let go. As I was very near the shore, 1 thought to swim onshore in the course of a stroke or two, as I used to swim so well, but soon found out my mistake. I was sinking almost like a stone, and hauling astern in deeper water, when I gave up all hopes of life, and begun to swallow some water. I found arope under my breast, so that I had not lost all my senses. I hauled upon it, and soon found one end fast to the side just where I went overboard, which gave me a little hope of life. So that when I got there, could not tell which was best, to call to the man-of-war's men to take me in, or to stay there and die, for my life and strength was allmoste exhausted ; but whilst I was thinking of this, touched bottam with my feet. Hope then sprung up, and I soon found another rope, leading

---

[1] 'Burtons,' a small tackle of two pulleys to be fastened anywhere at pleasure.—(Phillips' *Dictionary*, 1706). Now obsolete.

towards the head of the vessel in shoaler water, so that I veered upon one and hauled upon the other that brought me under the bowsprit, and then at times, upon the send of a sea, my feete was allmoste dry. I thought then I would soon be out of their way. Left go the rope, but as soon as I attempted to run, fell down, and as I fell, looking round aboute me, saw three men standing close by me. I know they were the man-of-war's men seeing for the boat, so I lyed there quiet for some little time, and then creeped upon my belly I suppose aboute the distance of fifty yards ; and as the ground was scuddy, some flat rock mixt with channels of sand, I saw before me a channel of white sand, and for fear to be seen creeping over it, which would take some time, not knowing there was anything the matter with me, made the second attempt to run, and fell in the same manner as before. My brother Charles being there, looking out for the vessel, desired some of Cawsand men to go down to see if they could pick up any of the men dead or alive, not ex-pecting ever to see me any more, allmoste sure I was ither shot or drowned. One of them saw me fall, ran to my assistance, and taking hold of me under the arm says, ' Who are you ? ' So as I thought him to be an enemy, made no answer. He said, 'Fear not, I am a friend ; come with me.' And by that time forth was two more come, which took me under both arms, and the other pushed me in the back, and so dragged me up to the town. I suppose it might have been about

C

the distance of the fifth part of a mile.   My strength
was allmoste exhausted ; my breath, nay, my life, was
allmoste gone.   They took me into a room where
there were seven or eight of Cawsand men and my
brother Charles, and when he saw me, knew me by my
great coat, and cryed with joy, ' This is my brother ! '
So then they immediately stript off my wet clothes,
and one of them pulled off his shirt from off him and
put on me, sent for a doctor, and put me to bed.
Well, then, I have thought many a time since what
a wonder it was.   The bone of my nose cut right in
two, nothing but a bit of skin holding it, and two
very large cuts in my head, that two or three pieces
of my skull worked out afterwards ; and after so long
laying on the deck with that very cold weather, and
being not alltogether drowned, but allmoste, I think, I
did not know I was wounded or loste any blood.
And now, my dear reader, I am going to show you the
hardening nature of sin.   When I was struggling in
the water for life I gave up all hope, I was dead in my
own mind ; nevertheless my conscience was so dead
asleep I thought nothing aboute Heaven or hell or
judgement ; and if I had died then I am sure I should
have awaked amongst devils and damned spirits.
See here this greate salvation and that of the Lord.
I have been very near drowned, I think, twice before
this, and have been exposed to many dangers many a
time in the course of time betwen the five years the
lugger was loste in the North Channel and this time,

privateering, smuggling, etc., but I think conscience never so dead as now. I stayed there that night and the next evening took chaise. My brother and me, and the docter came with us so far as Lostwithiel, and arrived at home the night after to brother Charles' house. I stayed there about six or seven days, until it was advertised in the papers, I think three hundred pounds for apprehending the Captain for three months from the date thereof, which set us all of alarm. So I moved from there to a gentleman's house at Marazion. I think I stayed there about two or three weeks, and from thence moved to Acton Castle,[1] as my brother John rented the farm, the famely not being there then, so that the keys and care of the house were left to his charge, and after a few days removed to Marazion again, then afraid of the shaking of a leaf. I think I might have stayed at Marazion for the course of a fortnight, and then went to the Castle again.[2] I used to half burn my coals by night in order that there should be no smoke seen in the day-time. In the course of about three months, after my wounds were nearly healed, I used to go at night to the King's Cove and there to drink grog, etc., with the

---

[1] Near Cuddan Point. It was built about 1775 by Mr. John Stackhouse, of Pendarves.

[2] It is said that the doctor who attended him at this time was always met on the road about a mile away by two men, who blind-folded him ; and in this way he was brought to the Castle, and so led back to the road again. A precaution to prevent him from giving information as to Harry Carter's hiding place.

Cove boys until the gray of the morning, convictions following me very sharp still at times. In my way home to my dreary lodgings, the larks flying up in the fields around me, warbling out their little beautiful notes, used to move me with envy, saying, ' These dear little birds answer the end they were sent in the world for, but me, the worst of all creatures that ever was made.' So that I have wished many a time I had been a toad, a serpent, or anything, so that I had no soul, for I know I must give an account for my conduct in this world. Likewayse there was a gray thrush that sang to me night and morning close to the house, which have preached to me many a sermon.

In the daytime I chiefly spent my time improving my learning on navigation, etc. I remember one Sabbath day, when I was at Marazion, I heard some people singing of hymns. I think they were Lady Huntingdon's people, when sincerely wished I had been one of them. I often [1] thought there was very great beauty in religion, and when I have been with others laughing and ridiculing the methodists, wished I had been one of them, whom I thought best of them. See what hypocrite was here. I remember aboute a year before this I went with my wife to Caerlean preaching, on the Sunday afternoon, where I stood as near as I could by the door. When the word fastened upon my mind, saying, ' Thou art the man.' So that I

[1] Spelt ' oughten ' in the manuscript. See note 1, p. 5.

was constrained to turn my face to the wall and weep
bitterly, with promises to mend my life, etc. But,
alas! I had not gone perhaps an hundred yards
from the house until I joined my old companions, so lost all my convictions. That was not
the only time by many when I have set up reso-
lutions in my own strength to serve the Lord,
etc. Well, then, in the course of this time, whilst at
this place, my wife would come to see me, and sometimes bring the child with her, and spend a day or
two, so that I passed my time pleasantly whilst she
was with me. I think it was in the latter end of
August my wife was taken very poorly in con-
sumption, being before of a delicate constitution, and
was allwayse obliged to come and go at night. I
think it was in the beginning of Oct$^{r.}$ in 1788
when I went to Helford to see her, in company with
a servant man to brother John, one night, as she
removed from her own house to be with her mother.
I found her in a very weak state, and as I expected
then soon to quit the country, I stayed with her
about two or three hours, when we took our final
farewell of each other, never expecting to see each
other no more in time. Oh, what a trying scene it
was, to leave her in flood of tears. So I arrived
home to my dreary solitude a little before day. I,
before then, was greatly distressed for her soul, and
through friends desired Uncle James Thomas to
visit her, so he did often. I think it was about

the 10 or 12 of the same month, when I was sitting upon a bench in one of the ground floors, bemoaning my sad estate, I began to say to myself, ' I have loste my liberty, my property ; I have loste my wife also '—as she was the same as dead to me then— so I thought that if her life were spared, it mattered little to me if I was to go to the West or East Indies, so that I could only hear from her by letters, would leave me some comfart. But that was taken away allso ; so that when I was cutt off from every comfart in this life, that I had not the least straw to lay hold of, I begun to see the emptiness and vanity of every- thing here below, and set up the resolution, God being my Helper, I will serve him the remnant of my days, so that I immediately fell to my knees and begun to say, 'Lord, have mercy upon me. Christe, have mercey upon me,' etc. ; and at that time I could not say the Lord's Prayer without form, if any man would give me my liberty, being so long living without prayer. So, then, as before time I used to divert myself in the daytime in looking at the ships and boats in the bay, the men and cattle working in the fields, etc., but now shut my eyes against them all ; and if I had business in the daytime to go to the top of the house, was with my eyes shut. So I went on with the above prayer, sometimes in hope of mercy, other- times loste allmoste all hope. Oct$^{r.}$ 24, in 1788, sailed from Mounts Bay for Leghorn in the ship 'George,' Capt$^{n.}$ Dewen, master. Was put on board

with a boate from the King's Cove, accompanied by
brother John, and I think I was allmoste like a dead
man ; thought little or nothing consarning my wife or
child, or anything in this world, but was earnestely
crying for mercy. I had a little cabin to myself to
lodge in, where there was only a single partition
between me and the men. At first it was a great
pain to me to hear them swearing, but after a little
while took very little notice of it. I had sume very
good books to read with me, but they seem to be
all locked up to me, as the natural man cannot
desarn the things of the Spirit of God, for they are
to be spiritualy desarned. I remember sumetimes
reading, when I could not understand, I should be so
peevish and fretfull that I could heave the book overboard. Then, oh, what a torment in my poor soul I
feeled. Then to think, surely the mercy of God is
clean gone from me. Oh, what burthen my life was
unto me. At them times I seldom prayed then less
in secret than twelve times a day and night, and
when I could pray with a little liberty, I should be in
hope of mercy, and at other times kneel down and
groan without one word brought to my remembrance,
then allmoste ready to give up all, saying, 'Surely
there is no mercy for me ; all my prayers is no use
at all, God pays no respect unto them ;' but still I
dare not give up praying. I could look back afterward and see I was all prayer. So I think I arrived
at Leghorn in the latter end of December, where I

passed my Christmas.   I think the first Sabbath
after I came there the Captn. asked me to go on
shore to church with him, as there was an English
church and clergyman there.   I gladly went.   The
minister being a good reader, I saw in his countenance much gravity and solemnity.   I said to
myself, ' Surely this is the man of God,' and thought
I was highly favoured to hear him.   The next
Sunday I gladly went again, but on coming on board
after the service was over, I was told that sacrament
days he did not scruple to go to the plays and
cards, etc., which poisoned my mind so with pre-
judice, I never went nomore.   In the course of all
this time I never meet with one person to give me
one word of advice consarning my soul, but I
laboured to keep myself to myself so much as
posable, still reading and praying with all diligence.
Well, then the Captn. got a freight there to go to
Barcelona, to load with brandy for New York in
America.   I was very glad when I heard of it, as I
heard that there was methodists there, in hope I
should fall in with sume of them to give me a word
of instruction.   So I think we sailed from Leghorn
in the latter end of Jany. in 1789.   The Lord still
continued to strive with me, sumetimes in hope of
salvation, other times allmoste ready to give up all
hope ; but I still was diligent in reading and prayer,
but I was so ignorant of the ways of salvation as I
was at the first time I began to pray.   I remember

on my passage there one day, scudding before the wind, very cold weather, and a very big sea, looking over the starn. I thought I should be very glad to be tyed in a rope and towed after the ship for a fortnight, if that would get me into the favour of God. But, alas! I know all such works would not merit anything from God as salvation. I arived at New York on the 19 April in '89, and aboute ten or twelve days before I arived there, I was taken with a violent inflammation in one of my eyes, so I could see very little on that eye   and the other much afected allso. So after two or three days being there, there came a glasar[1] on board to put in a pane of glass in the cabin windows. And as the Captn· and mate was not presant, I thought it was my time to enquire out the methodists, and as shame allways hunted me much, I begun to ask him aboute the defrante persuasions of people there; at laste I asked, 'Is there any of Mr. Wesly's methodists here?' He answered, 'There is many.' I asked him, 'Do you know any of them?' He answered, 'Yes, many of them.' I asked, 'What sort of people are they?' thinking, if he gave them a bad carakter, to say no further. His answer, 'They are a good sorte of people,' so then I asked him, 'Do you know the precher?' He said, 'I do, and I go to hear him sometimes.' I said, 'Then I shall be obliged to you if you will send your little boy with me to show me the precher's

---

[1] Glazier.

house.' So after he stared a little at me, said, ' If you will stay a little until I have done this job, I will ither go with you myself or git sume person that shall.' So that encouraged me very much, set me in high spirits, and after a little further discourse, he told me his wife was a methodist, and soon after took me to his house, where the dear woman received me very kindly. And when she know I wanted to speak to the precher, she asked me if I did belong to the connection in *England*. I answered, ' No, but I wants to speak to the precher.' She said, ' To-night is publick meeting night. I will go with you a half hour sooner, when we shall find Mr. Dickinson home.' So accordingly we went together, where I found the dear man and his wife in the kitchen. As soon as I looked at him, I said to myself, ' This is the man I wants to see ; this is the man of God.' I said, ' Sir, I should be glad to speak a few words with you.' So as there was no persons presant but his wife and the good woman that come with me, said, ' Say on.' I said, ' To yourself, if you please, sir.' So he took me into a small parlor and said, ' What do you want of me ? ' I said, ' Sir, I am an Englishman, and belong to a ship in the harbour. I know I am a great sinner, and as I am informed you belongs to Mr. Weseley's people, I want to know what I must do.' He looked at me and said, ' Do you think God would be just to send you to hell ? ' I was surprised at such a question, did not know what answer to make. Then he begun to say to this purpose, that Christe come to seek and to save that which was lost, etc. He likewayse asked me, 'Do you pray?' I said, 'Yes, a little.' 'Do you fast too?' said he. I said, 'No, sir.' So, after asking me a few more questions he said, 'There is a publick prayer meeting here this evning, you may stay if you please.' So I thought he paid me a very great compliment. I thanked him, and when the time come, that dear woman took me to the *meeting* house and put me in a place to sit down. So after they had sung and prayed, the precher gave an exhortation, and I thought all to me, so that I was a little comfarted; and after the meeting was ended, the dear woman took me by the hand, as I was half blind, and lead me home to her own house; and the good glasar, her husband, lead me on board, with a strict charge not to fail coming to see them to-morrow. So I gladly accepted of the invitation, and when I came there she had brought one of the class leaders and a good old woman to meet me, who gave me great encouragement to seek the Lord. My eye still getting worse, and as I could not get leeches as I used to do at home, applyed to a doctor, and he cutt the small blood-vessels of the apple of my eye, and so lett the blood out. So as the ship was going to Baltimore to load, I thought if I went in her I should be in danger to lose the sight of one eye if not both, as both was much afected. So, then, I concluded to stay there, where I attended all the ordinance; some place to go to every night. And I think it was aboute the 1 of May when I was asked if I would have a note of admittance to meet in class. I thought it to be the greatest compliment I ever received in all my life, and gladly accepted it ; so that when the leader asked my name, as he took me in surprize, I said, ' Harry.' He said, ' Is that your sir name ? ' I said, ' Yes.' Then he asked, ' What is your Christian name ? ' I said, ' Henry.' So the people called me, sume ' Mr. Harry ' and sume ' Captin Harry,' as the sailors I come with *caled me* ' Captn. Harry ' ; so that in the course of a very little time I got more acquaintance with them dear people. I could see afterwards I was hungering and thirsting after righteousness, but sometimes in hope of mercy, othertimes allmoste ready to give up all. I used to walk out of town every morning in sume solitary place to myself to read and pray ; and I know since that time if I wanted to know when the clock struck twelve in order to go home, that the family should not wait for me for dinner—I did hardely know much better when the clock had done striking no more than when it begun—I had not the time to count two, for all my soul was in a blaze of prayer. I think in the begining of May, Doctor Cook[1] come there to hold confarence. I wished to make myself known unto him, but was afraid, as

[1] Thomas Coke, LL.D. ; he was ordained Bishop or Superintendent of the American Methodist Societies by John Wesley in 1784.

at that time I know very little aboute the methodists
—afraid of the shaking of a leaf. And for all[1] I
was so highly favoured with so much helps and means
I could form no idea of justifying faith. Sometimes
I thought I should here as a man's voice to speak
unto me, other times think to see something with my
bodily eyes, other times think as if my body should
be changed. I have thought many times that there
never was one so ignorant as I was in the ways of
salvation. Sometimes, if I could weep a little under
a sarmon, or in a prayer meeting, I should have some
hope I was in the way, and sumetimes feel the
drawings of the Father, which would give me sume
encouragement and hope ; other times, if I saw any
persons weeping by me, should complain of the hardness of my heart, and be allmoste ready to give up
all. Nevertheless I still continued praying—I supose
seldom less than twelve times in a day—and sometimes
think whether the hindrance was because I missed
naming myself. Well, then, I have thought many a
time since of my unwillingness to belief, for all I was
blessed with so many helps and means. The prechers,
and aboute six or seven people in particular, took me
by the hand and was like fathers, mothers, brothers,
and sistars, so that I often in the afternoon amongst
sume of them dear women and the prechers, drinking
tea, &c. ; and if I should sit with them more than an

---

[1] This expression, which occurs several times in the following pages,
is common in West Cornwall in the sense of 'although.'

half hour without sume of them should ask me something of the state of my mind, I should be so much
dejected, and say to myself, 'Surely I am beneath
the least of their notice; how can I expect the least
of their notice?' And I remember one day went to the
hospital to preching. When the preching was over,
the two prechers, Mr. Morld and Mr. Cloude, in their
way home, I drew nigh to them; thought to have
some conversation with them, and as they used to
make so free with me, then only spoke as I thought
coldly. I was so much dejected in my own mind,
I thought I was the worst creature that ever was born,
and that allmoste all things cryed vengance against
me. Another time I remember I went to the
precher's house to inquire after Mr. Cooper, he not
being there that presant, and as I went out to one
door he came in to the other, I not seeing him.
Mr. Morld said to him, 'Brother Carter was here
inquiring after you.' I heard him, and was immediately struck with wonder to think a such man as he
should be so humble as to call a such poor creature
as me, brother. So these was some of the ways I
was tryed. Some times up, sume times down, sume
times in hope and sume times allmoste ready to give
up. Notwithstanding all this I continued still
in prayer, and I remember when walked the streets I
was like one with his eyes shut, crying for salvation,
and likewayse crying to the Lord that there might

nothing take my attention or the least of my afection
from Him in this world. I think I was there aboute
three or four weeks, when I was asked why I did not
go to sacrament. I answered, 'I am unworthy.' The
person answered, 'You are the very person that is
worthy.' So as he could not prevail upon me to go,
he told the prechers of it, and after class meeting on
the Sabbath morning, as they was going to a friend's
house to breakfast, asked me to go with them. They
soon opened their commission, and asked me to come
to the sacrement to-day. I answered, I could not.
They asked my reason. I said, 'Him that eateth and
drinketh unworthy, eateth and drinketh his own
damnation,' and immediately I burst out in a flood of
tears, and desired the company to pray for me. The
whole large company kneeled down, and prayed for
me with great powar, so that I had not the only wet
face by many in the company, and after prayer took
me to reason, so I consented to go. And I went with
much fear and trembling. I feeled nothing particular
in the ordinance, but ever after continued to go. I
think it was in the beginning of June I begun to
abstain from eating, and as I eate to the full before,
I slackoned a little every meal. I was afraid to fast
for fear the family should take notice of me; and
aboute this time I sent home for sume money, then
thinking to set on a shop in Co. with Robt. Snow,
then thinking to leave my bones there. So I still

went on sume times thinking I was getting into lukewarm state, other times a little hope of mercy, and sume times allmoste despair of all mercy. But I remember 19 July I went to preaching as usual, when, as the preacher was pointing out the odiousness of sin, and the hartfeelt sorrow that a true penitent soul feeled for it, he mentoned of a woman that had a cancer cutt out of her breast a few days before, and when she was asked if the pain was not very great, her answer was, 'Not so great as when I was under convictions for sin.' I immediately concluded I was out of the way. I had hardley the least hope left of Christ, Heaven, or happyness. So in my way home in company with Mr. Cooper, a little before we parted he said, 'Captⁿ·, what is the matter? You seem to be lowspirited to-night.' I answered, 'Yes, and well I may.' He said, 'What then is the matter?' I said, 'Did you not hear Mr. Morel saying aboute the woman that had the cancer cutt out of her breast, and I am sure I am not in the way, I never feeled such pain at all,' etc. He said, 'I am sure you are in the way, and then begun to repeat the promises, etc. I thought I had heard the same promises repeated hundreds of times before, but never in such manner as at presant. Hope sprung up that the blessing was very near to me.

I went home to my lodgings, and after prayer opened the Hymbook to—

Salvation, oh the joyfull sound,
What music to our ears ;

> A sovereign balm for every wound,
>   A cordial for our fears.
> Glory, honour, etc, etc.[1]

I was allmoste ready to fly away. I went to bed, but did hardly sleep all the night, praying and praising God. Never the less in all this I did not believe that my sins was pardoned, but I hope God would do it, and that soon. In the morning went to the man of God, told him how I feeled, to which he gave me great encouragement. The next night went to preaching aboute two miles out of town. I was still very comfartable, but could not believe. The next day being 21, aboute two or three o'clock in the afternoon, I went to pray that God would show me the hindrance that stood between him and my soul, and that he would show me by that man of God, or by some other means. After I rose up from my knees I went to the man of God. He saw me coming, and asked me with a smile, 'Well, Captain, how is it with you now?' I answered, 'I have been just now praying that God would show me the hindrance that stands between him and my soul, and take it away from me.' He answered in his usual pleasant way, 'Nothing at all, Captain, only unbelief; but I would advise you to spend moste of this afternoon in prayer, that God would show you under the sarmon, or by some other means, before you go to bed,' etc. So I did accord-

---

[1] This is one of Dr. Watts's hymns. It was not included by John Wesley in the Hymn-book which he published in 1790.

ing to his direction, and in the evning went to preching in great expectation. And when Mr. Morel delivered his text from the 15 chapter St. John, 'Abide in me and I in you,' and as he went on a little, I thought, surely this is for me. Hope sprung up ; but after a little further I thought Mr. Cooper had been telling the precher of what I had told him, which set me in doubting. But after he went on a little further, I said to myself, 'Whether he have told him or not, it is for me,' and I believed in that moment, so that I rejoiced with joy unspeakable and full of glory. As soon as the sarvice was ended, lest Satan should get an advantage over me, I told the precher what the Lord had done for me, and immediately Mr. Cooper, so that we rejoiced greately together, to which the latter told me, 'You must go in the morning to such and such a ones' (mentioned six or seven houses), 'and tell them what the Lord have done for you, and forget not to sing and pray with them. So I went according to his order, and told them that I had received the comforter, so that we had a happy morning together. Well, then, I went on my way rejoicing, no doubts, no fears, nither hardly a temptation, until the end of ten or twelve days. So then I went on, sume times on the mount with Peter and John, some times in doubts and fears ; and if I did not allwayse find my mind in a blaze of prayer unto God, I frequent used to say to myself, 'Now I am surely getting into a lukewarm

state,' and so write bitter things against myself. Aboute
this time I begun to fast once a week, until aboute
four o'clock in the afternoon, and abstain to nearly
half my fill. I think it was in the later end of Augst
when I received a letter from my mother-in-law
consarning my wife's death. I soon begun to reason
if she was gone happy or not, so that in the course of
a few days after I used to go out by night, and looking up towards heaven, wishing and praying to see
her vision, or to know by some means whether she was
gone happy or not. And one night, before I went to
bed, I prayed earnestely to the Lord if he would show
me by dream or by vision. So that night I dreamed
I was amongst serpents and vipars, and the worst of
venemest beasts, that I had the hardest struggels to
get clear of them, so when I awaked I was in a lake
of sweat from head to foot. Then I thought I had
not done according to the will of God. I continued
in that state, with my harp hanged upon the willows,
could not sing one note for a thousand worlds for all
so much delight I took in it in times past, keep it all
this time to myself, so that I got myself into such
wilderness state that I could hardly tell if I was in
the favour of God or not. But I think it was to the
end aboute fourteen days I opened my mind to Mrs.
Snow, who said, ' By your own account your wife had
good morals, and she *had* also the preachers and people
to pray and instruct her ; I have a good hope she is
gone happy. Nevertheless, whether or not, you must

leave that to God, it is a business you must have nothing at all to do with ; and if you continue to go on in this way, I am in doubt as you are in danger to lose all your Religion.   So we kneeled down and she prayed for me, and immediately I went to a prayer meeting.   The first hymn was,

> My God, the spring of all my joy,
> The life of my delights, etc.

I sung with a loud voice but with a wet face, so that the temptation left me.   Glory be to God for dear friends, etc.   So I went on as before, some times happy and other times in doubts and fears, but still getting a little strength.

I think it was aboute this time that I left of drinking water, and I think it was in the beginning of September I concluded in my mind to quit the town and go to Baltimore ; and as there was a ship bound there I spoke for a passage, and got most things ready for the voyage.   But oh! what a tryal it was to me to think of leaving of my New York friends, where the Lord had helped me in such abundant manner, and then to go 700 miles from there to a place and people I knew nothing of.   I begun to reason as before with the enemy of my soul ' Surely at last I shall become a castaway, surely Is hall be stripped of all my Religion !'   I suppose no man can conceive the misery I felt in my own mind for the course of aboute ten or twelve days; I have thought since that I never had a greater tryal. But to the end of this time one night I went to preching, where Mr. Asbery,[1] with his great loud voice, gave out this hymn—

> Tho' troubles assail and dangers afright,
> If friends all should fail and foes all unite,
> Yet one thing assures us, what ever betide,
> I trust in all dangers the Lord will provide, etc. etc.[2]

I never heard that hymn before, and as he went on I was filled with such faith and love I could trust and not be afraid ; it matterd nothing to me where I went, as I believed that God would be with me. I never opened my mind to no person in the course of all this time, but I was thinking to the same day I sailed, or the day before, and that only to desire one of my friends when my money came from England to remitt it unto me. But at that time, as I was so happy in God, and could trust him with both soul and body, I thought I could trust his servant allso. So I begun and opened all my mind to my Father Cooper, told him who and what I was, and how I came there, and all my reason I had to quit the town, which was, as my right name was H. Carter, and as I hailed as H. Harry, I thought if I entered into business I must at

---

[1] Francis Asbury. He was sent to America by John Wesley in 1771, and was elected joint Superintendent with Dr. Coke at the Conference held at Baltimore in 1784. He was the only English preacher who remained in America during the War of Independence.

[2] This is one of the ' Olney ' hymns by Cowper and Newton.

times have business upon the wharves,[1] amongst the shipping ; and if I ever meet any person that know me I should be branded as a hypocrite, and hurt my partner and sadly wound the cause of God. He answered and said, 'Captain, as that is the cause, I think you need not leave the place. If you think proppar, I'll speak to the prechars and your leader, and appoint to meet to one of your friend's houses one afternoon, where, I think, we shall be able to settle all the business, but you must not be presant.' Accordingly they meet all together, those I was moste particular acquainted with, so he opened the business. They all joined together, and said, ' He did this when in a natural state, not meaning to wrong or defraud any man, for personal safety ; and when we hear anyone call him "Captain Harry" or "Mr. Harry," we must say his surname is Carter, as it is the custom in England where there is two Captains of one family, the one is called after his Christian name.' So my old friend delayed no time, but soon come with this full account to me, where I rejoiced in my great deliverer. I could not then doubt but this was the Lord's doings, and it was marvellous in my eyes, so that the report soon spread aboute the town. But moste of them, as they begun with 'Captain Harry,' so continued ; and I thought, tho' their love was so great to me before, it

---

[1] Spelt 'worps' in the manuscript, which is dialect pronunciation. Cf. 'sharps' for 'shafts' (of a cart), and 'vycicle' for 'bycicle,' which are both common.

was increased if possible tenfold more so; so then I concluded in my mind to stay, and thought to live and die there, and went on as before, watching and praying, frequaintely complaining of my littleness of love, weakeness of Faith, etc., until aboute the 19 of December, when I went to class meeting on the Sabbath morning. Providence sent one there from the County of Durham, in England, whose name was Hodg-. son. He lately come to town in company with two excellent men from the same place, and as he being a stranger, the leader desired him to speake to the people. So he begun, saying how and when he was convinced of sin, when he was converted, and when he was sanctified unto God; and after, exhorted all that believed to only believe and see the salvation of God, and with this language, ' all things in Christe is now ready, all the fitness he requires is to feel the need of him.' So he preached a presant and full salvation unto us. Such language I never heard before with no man. Now in the course of this time I had been there Religion was not in a very prospras state, few [1] convinsed and very few converted unto God, but the people going on still in a steady state, so that we never heard sanctification preached, or seldom prayed for, in publick, and amongst the whole of the methodists that was there at that time, aboute, as well as I can remember, 260 in all, and only two persons out of the whole number that did perfess and enjoy the blessing of sanctification—my

[1] Spelt ' feve ' in the manuscript. Cf. note 2, p. 3.

Father Cooper was one, and an old woman the other. So that I thought if I could receive that blessing to the end of three or four years, I thought it would be a blessing indeed, etc. So then, after the meeting was ended, as Mr. Hodgson and me lodged in the same part of the town, went in company together. He begun to ask me who I was, etc., so that I gave him a true description of how long I had been in town, and what the Lord had done for me since I had been there. When I had done speaking, he said, ' Well, my brother, be thankfull for what the Lord have done for you, and ask for more ;' and some thing in this way, 'Go on to perfection, it is the will of God, even your sanctification. Do you believe these things ? ' I answered, ' I believe in the doctrine of sanctification, but I cannot believe the promise is to me.' He asked for what reason. I said, ' I am a poor egnarant person, and it is not more than five months since I am justified, and there is a great number of excellent men and women in this town that is usefull to their fellow creatures in praying in publick, visiting the sick, instructing the ignorant, etc., they do not perfess this blessing at all, and how can I expect it, who am good for nothing, and so unworthy and unfit for it.' He answered, ' All the fitness he requires is to feel the need of him. The promise is for you ; only believe, and see the salvation of God,' etc. So the discourse I had with him set my soul all of a flame, the blessing seemed to be nigh me. I went home and fell to my knees in prayer. I thought

I was just ready to laye hold of it, but unbelief
hindered me ; but the hope of the blessing being so
very nigh, made me rejoice in abundant manner. I
was very happy all that day and the next day also,
still in earnest expectation to receive the blessing.
But the day following went to a prayer meeting, being
on 21 December, where I meet Mr. Hodgson provi-
dentely, and after the meeting he asked me to go
home to his house with him. I gladly embraced the
opportunity, and after a little conversation by his
fireside the Lord enabled me to believe in him for
full salvation. I immediately told him, saying, ' Glory
be to God, I do believe.' So after we sung and prayed,
he said, ' You must go in the morning and tell your
friends of what the Lord have done for you ; this
blessing may not be given for your sake only, but for
others also. So I parted with him, and went home,
jumping,[1] and leaping, and praising of God. And
the next morning, according to his order, I went from
house to house, and told the six or seven familes that
I was moste particular acquainted with what the
Lord had done for my soul, so that we rejoiced
greately together, they farmely believed the report.
And I have thought many times since, as if I hard
them say, ' Now we see God have no respect of persons.
This poor ignorant Englishman have been here with
us only a few months, have been justified and sanc-

---

[1] Spelt ' youmping ' in the manuscript. Cf. ' yest ' for ' just,' note 1,
p. 1.

tified, and surely if this blessing is to be attained too, we will never rest until we receive it.' So that the preachers and people were all in alarm. In the course of a few days there were new prayer meetings set up upon allmoste every quarter of the town, so that in a very little time the Chapel would scarcely hold half of the people, and the Lord begun to pour a lot of his spirit upon the people in a wonderful manner—some crying for mercy, others standing up rejoicing and praising of God that they know their sins was forgiven them ; likewayse others rejoicing, saying that God spake the second time, ' Be clean,' and cast out all their inbred sin ; and oh, what a glorious work was there. I know one of my friends going home from a prayer meeting one night, aboute two or three o'clock in the morning, called to another friend's house, knocked him out of bed, and told him that God cleansed him from all unrighteousness. They both joined in prayer, and they wrasled with God until the other experienced the same blessing allso. So that with the noise and brusel [1] of the people the world seemed as it were turned upside down. The Calvinests, Baptists, Universalists, Quakers, with the people of the Establish Church, all seemed to rise up in arms against it. Sume said the devel was amongst the methodists, sume one thing, sume another ; but the work continued to go on in a glorious manner, so that in the course of aboute two or three months the

[1] ? ' Bustle.'

society increased from aboute 260 to more than 500. It was then good times indeed, praise be to God. I have had the pleasure to see many revivals since, but I think I never saw greater heroes for the work then my dear friends in New York ; and I think the people there then was sumething like the primitive Christians, going from house to house in fellowship one with another, declaring the wonderfull works of God. Well, then, I am now going to return to myself. I think it was in the beginning of January, in 1790, when there was a meeting set up caled the ' Select Bands,' meant for those that was sanctified, and those believers that was pressing hard after it might join if they pleased. So I think there was aboute twenty that perfess sanctification joined, and about ten more that was crying after it. I think that was a scool indeed, to hear so many sensible men and women to stand up to tell of their experience from the begining to the presant, and I never was a greater wonder to myself than to be permitted amongst such people, as I was the youngest in the way and the moste ignorant of them all. So I still continued in all the ordinesses,[1] using not less secreat prayer than when I begun to seek the Lord, my soul moste times in a blaze of prayer.

I think it was in aboute the middle of January when I went one morning to the preachar's house in company with Mr. Coopar, where there was sevrall of the leaders, consulting where they should hold

[1] Ordinances.

prayer meetings, and how they should car[1] them on. I went home to my lodgings, and seating by the fire I begun first to reason, saying, 'Everyone is imployed, all have sume thing to do exepting me, and I am good for nothing, no use to society, but as a dead dog in the way.

Well, then, as I was a long time in expectation to have remittance from home, my money being done, and being in debt about 38 shillings for my board, I said to my creditor, 'I have gave up all hope of having any money from home, I muste begin to work aboute sumething, but what or where I know not. If I work in town the people will brand me for a deceiver, as I have said I have sume property and sent home for sume, so I fear it would much hurt the cause of Christ. I should be glad to have your advice in the case.' He answered, 'What you owes me is but a trifal, you need not go anywhere to work on my account. You are welcome to stay a month or two longer, perhaps your money will come ; and if not, do not make yourself uneasy aboute it.' But, however, my friend Hodgson aboute that time went upon Long Island to live, so that I spoke to him for lodgings and went with him, thinking I should be out of the way of censure. So the 12 of June I car'd my little sea bed there, and laid it in one corner of his room as he had nither steed[2] for me; so

[1] 'Carry'; dialect.
[2] 'Bedstead.' 'Stead' would be pronounced 'steed' in West Cornish dialect.

the next morning, being 13, went to work to a farmer aboute a mile and half from the little town where I lived, and was sent to the field to hoe Indian corn in company with a negro. The work was very strange unto me, but soon after begun fell into discourse with him, and I rejoiced to hear he belonged to New York society. We worked the forenoon in the field together, where I was pleased and profited with his conversation ; the afternoon being hard rain, we worked shifting of straw, etc., in the barn, when come the farmer, as I could not mow hay, etc., paid me my wages, and directed me in my way home to a cousin of his, whom I caled upon, and he told me to come the next morning. Accordingly I did so, who sent me in a field to do the same work, when aboute seven or eight o'clock I was joined with a man to work with me, who was part owner of the field. I worked until breakfast time, when I was caled in to breakfast. I could eate nothing, but drink a little milk, the same to dinner. The man that worked with me, as he could do much more work than me, desired me not to work to hard, but by three or four o'clock the blood was running between my fingers, and my body so weak, all moste ready to drop down. The man that was with me asked me no questions consarning who or what was, but a little before we left work went to a publick house and brought me a little rum and water, and desired me to drink again and again. I gladly took a very little of it, and should

have taken more, but I thought, as he know me to be
a methodist, he did it in order to trap me ; but I saw
after the man had no such desire, so I gladly received
it with thankfullness both to God and him.   So I
went home rambling, with a tired body, as one that
was much intoxicated.   The next morning went to
the same place again, but wore gloves to hide my
bleeding hands ; and as their hours was from aboute
sun rising, and stop a little to breakfast and dinner,
and work until sun set, and as my body was wasted
and weakened before with much fasting and absti-
nence, and had hardly dirted my finger scarcely for
nearley twenty years before, my body was allmoste
ready to crush under the burden.   Oh, what a change
was this indeed!   And as I used before to pray not less
than twelve times in a day in secreat, I had no opertunity
at that time but a few minuts before I went to work,
and find a little house or sume bye corner to breack-
fast and dinner ; and when I got home in the evning,
where the family was allmoste ready to go to bed.
But I can realy say, to the glory of God, I never
was so happy in all my life as I was at that *time*.
So I staid there two or three days to finish that *job*,
and after put in a field to work to myself some
distance from the house, and furder[1] from my home,
where my employer told me, 'You may lodge here if
you will.' I gladly accepted the offer, and the first
night I was took into a room in one end of the farm

---

[1] 'Further' ; dialect.

house and showed my bed, where there was an old
negro woman, and a little black boy with her. I
looked at my bed, the room, and my company, and I
think I never saw a meaner bed in all the course of
my life. Stripped off my clothes and turned in, in
full expectation that they was going to sleep with me,
as I saw no other bed or place else for them.
But whilst I was thinking of this, I saw there in one
cornar of the room a little ladder, where they both
went up together. I was there, I think, three or four
days in that field to myself, and I think it was the
second day, aboute eleven o'clock, I stood in the field
and leaned upon my hoe, and could not tell whether
I should drop down under my burthen or stand any
longer, the sun allmoste over my head, the wind very
little, and took hardely anything to sustain nature.
And I worked harder than perhaps I was required to,
and that for two reasons—the one for fear that they
should know I was a broken *gen*telman, and if
known, I should not have work to *do*. *The* other, I
must do justice unto my employer. Wilst I was thus
at a stand, calling to the L*ord* for help, I saw a light
shone brighter then the light of the sun, that filled me
with such faith and love, I went on again like a giant
refreshed with new wine, praising and blessing of
God. Oh, what happy times I had every moment.
After I had done the field, he had no work more for
me, so I returned home and got work a day or two
in a place. I keept all what I feeled to myself, no

murmuring, no complaining; but when my dear friends in New York come to hear of it, they agreed together to contribute to my maintenance, and take me off from there, and sent me word to be home one day, as they were coming to see me. Accordingly the day came, when six or seven women come according to promise, and after sume conversation opened their business, but in a very feeling manner. I thanked them, and said, ' I surely am not too good to work ; I have read of sume that have worked for their own bread that I am unworthy to wipe their shoes or snuff their candle.' So we passed the afternoon together in singing and praying. I saw them to the boate, where they made me promise not to fail to come to see them every Sunday, and, if possible, Saturday night.

After three or four days, working a day in a place, I went to work with a farmer near the place I worked before, where I went to hoe Indian corn with five or six negero slaves. They behaved unto me very civil indeed, desired me not to work too hard; and as the poorest workman amongst them could far out do me and do my best, but one or other allwayse helped me on, so that I kept *close* up with them. I was, as well as I can remem*ber*, with them six or seven days, and that time sleeped in a hay loft.[1] My suffering was not all over as yet; I could eate very little, and in the morning, when I

---

[1] Spelt ' laght ' in the manuscript. Cf. note 1, p. 5.

went to work, allmoste so sore and so tired as in the
evning ; and I could hardly say I could sleep at all,
at times just forget myself only.   All this time nither
master nor any man ever asked me who or what I
was, they only know I was an English man.   They
all treated me very civily, and when they had done
with me they would ask me my demands.   My answer
was, 'What you please'; so they allwayse gave me
the same as another common labourer.   Aboute this
time I was asked to go with a mason to repair a mill
dam ; it was to be repaired with turf, and I had a
small flatt bottam boat to carry the turf across the
pool.   So I went with him upon this conditions, if I
could do the work, to give me what he pleased.   I
expected at first he was to be allwayse with me, but
just showed me my work and left me to myself, only
sume times come to see me, once in the course of two
or three days.   I then lodged and boarded myself to
friend Hodgson's.   The place was in a bottam,[1] in
mirey ground, and the weather very hot, that the
sweat would run over me in large drops, as if any
person was heaving water upon me.   I think I went
to work aboute sun rising in the morning, I suppose
aboute five o'clock, stop aboute half hour to breakfast,
only an hour to dinner, and then work until sun set, I
suppose aboute seven.   My breakfast and dinner was
a piece of bread I car'd with me, and I went to a farm
house for a little milk.   When my employer come to

---

[1] The ordinary word for 'a valley,' in West Cornwall.

see me, he would moste times bring with him a little
rum and a cup, and as there was a will [1] close by,
'Come,' said he, 'rest yourself a little ; let us go and have
a drink together.'   What a change indeed was workd
upon me ; before time, when I was, as it were, a gentelman, I could not touch a dram before dinner upon any
account.   But then how glad and how thankfull I was
to receive it.   But after the first fortnight or three
weeks my bones was become a little more hardened,
my sufferings was not alltogether so much, and I have
thought many a times when my sufferings was to the
greatest, that if it was the will of Providence I would
gladly continue in the same all the days of my life.
So every Sabbath day I went to New York to see
my friends in the morning and return back again in
the evning.

I think it was in the later end of July when
Mr. Dawson, one of them English men I before
mentioned that came from the County of Durham,
came over to inform me that if I would go home
there was a vessel that would be ready in the course
of a week's time, and he was going to England.   I
th*anked* him and went to New York, and asked the
advice of my friends. They all, as the voice of one man,
said, 'Surely this is the Lord's doing ; go, the Lord
will be with you.   We believe that it will not be in
the power of man to hurt you, but you must not
think it strange if you receive strong tryals from the

---

[1] A ' well '; dialect pronunciation.

Captain.' The Captain was an English man that come there from the West Indies, and had been in town for, I suppose, six or seven weeks ; a man that did profess Religion, and did at times stand up in publick as a preacher, but of Calvinist principles. And as I know him before, I went and asked him for a passage, then fully believing it was my duty, and I thought I could trust the Lord with my both soul and body. So he was quite agreeable, and then, as I was not acquainted with the man, opened all my mind unto him, notwithstanding for all the hints I had concarning him before. So he asked me if I was a navigator, and if I could work, etc. I answered I had my quadrant and books with me. So I agreed with him to be landed in Mounts Bay, or close to the East of the Lizard Point, and then returned back to Long Island, and told my employer I was going at home. He desired me to stay a few days longer with him to finish the job, to which I con-sented. And I think aboute the 3 or 4 of August, when we settled our accounts, he paid me very handsomely. I returned to New York. I paid off all my debts and bought myself sevrall little *seafar*ing clothes for the voyage, and I think I had four pence in *coppe*rs left. Well, then, here was a change in deed—from *such* hard labour to ease again. So I staid there with my dear friends, going from house to house as before. I think I was all-wayse rejoicing and praysing of God, and still using the same self-denial by abstaining from food as before time, and not only then, but allso when I was to my hardest labour. I staid there until the 13 August, when took breakfast with my old and first friend the glasar, and after breakfast he took a dollar out of his pocket and said, 'I insist on you to accept of it.' I thanked him, and I took it, so went on board, and that day got to an anchor in Sandyhook, and the next morn sailed for England with a fair wind and fair weather. The vessel was a small sloop aboute 40 tons,[1] bought by the Captain then in New York, but the papars draw'd in the mate's name, under cover him being an American. The cargo was coopers' timber, and the whole crew was the Captain, mate, two boys, Mr. Dawson, and myself. I keept one watch with the biggest boy, I suppose aboute 16 or 17 years old ; and the mate keept the other watch with the other boy, I suppose aboute 13 or 14 year old. We was not more then a day or two at sea until Satan begun to rage and roar. The Captain set his face against me. Try my best I could do nothing to please him. He pretended to know all things, but did hardly know anything of the sea or business. Then I thought of what I was told by my friends in New York, so that I was not the leaste disappointed. I acted in the capacity of steward and as cabin boy, to bring all things to his hand as a gentelman, and if there were anything

---

[1] Old measurement.

short I stayed without it ; so that I had plenty to do to try to please him, besides keep my regular watch on deck night and day. We had a fair wind until we came upon the banks of Newfoundland. Then the wind took us ahead and blow fresh for a little time. The vessel made some water upon one tack ; he said, ' We will bear up for Boston.' I think, for all he was a professor of Religion, I never saw a man more afraid of his life in all my life. I thought that if we put in to Boston I never should fetch home in that vessel. I opposed him, and said, ' There is no danger, I will engage to keep the pump in my watch.' Mr. Dawson said, ' I will keep it in the other,' tho' he know nothing of the sea. The mate then joined us, and amongst us all gained our point, so that soon after we had a fair wind again.

We had moste times publick prayers in the morning, sume times Mr. Dawson and sume times him, but still continued with his face set against me, and poor Mr. Dawson dare not speak one word in my favour, as he was full so much afraid of him as I was. And the two poor boys, I think in the hardness of my times it never was in my power to treat two dogs as he treated them. So one day, after we come in to soundings, I said, ' The Land's End bears so and so, it is time for you to alter your course if you land me there.' So as he pretended to keep a reckning he said to the contrary, but never let us see his journal, the mate and me, within

two or three miles of each other,[1] so that I thought
he had no mind to land me in the Mounts Bay,
according to promise, the weather being fair.   Saw a
sail, and as it was not the first time by many, said to
me, as I had the helm, ' Bear down to speak with him.'
I did so.   He said, ' Keep her so and so.'   I said, 'Sir, if
you keep her so, you never will speak with him.'   He
begun to belch out, ' What is that to thee ? I say keep
her so.'   So as I had given up all hope of being
landed there, I thought it was time to take a little
courage.   I left go the helm and said, ' Keep her so
your self, if you please,' and I immediately went
below and turned in in my cabin.   In the course of
a little time he came down and said sume thing to me
in a very surly manner.   I answered, 'Sir, you have not
behaved unto me as a man since I have been with
you.   I have answered every end I engaged with
you for, and much more so, and now I see you are
entirely off your word with me, as you know you
was to land me in the Mounts Bay, or a little to the
East of the Lizard.'   He begun to bale out, ' Thou
doste profess the spirit of Christe, but thou haste the
spirit of the devil,' and so on in a great rage, my poor
friend Dawson presant fearing and trembling but
dare not speak one word ; and I have thought that
good man suffered during the voyage much more
on my account than I did myself.   So I did not
render railing for railing, said nothing, or very little

[1] *I.e.,* in their reckoning as to the position of the vessel.

more. This was in the evning, and in the course
of aboute half hour after, when he come to himself,
he came to me and said in a very good humour, ' I
should be glad if you would turn out and come on
deck, I wants to speak with you.' So he took me forward on the bow out of the sight and hearing of any
person, and said sumething to this purpose : ' I hope
you'll think nothing of all that is past, and I am
going to tell you why I cannot be to my word with
you to land you in the Mounts Bay. I sarved my time
to a hatter in London, and as there was a brig there
loaden with hats and other goods, I took her away under
the pretence of being supercargo, etc., unknown to the
owners. I sold the vessel and cargo in the West
Indies, bought the sloop you see me come to New
York in, sold that sloop there, and bought what we
are in at present. I told you and others I was bound
to London, but I meant to go to Dunkerk and send
for my wife to London. I mean to sell my cargo and
then to return to New York again, for if I am known in
any part of England I shall be apprehended and hanged.
So now let me beg you to keep it a secret. And I have
the favour likewayse, as you know there is no draft for
the Channel on board, I knows nothing of the Channel,
and the mate quite unacquainted, let me beg you to do
your best to car the vessel to Dunkerk.' I answered, ' I
will do every thing in my powar,' etc. These was the
tener of our discourse, etc. So that when he had
finished, I thought I was allmoste lost in wonder and

astonishement. I thought my case was bad, but his tenthousands times worse. So I turned to work again with a willing mind, knowing nothing should happen unto me against the knowledge of God, nither without his permision, and I believed all things should work together for my good, and so went on my way, rejoicing and praising of God.

The weather still very fair and a fair wind. The next morning saw the Start Point, and so made the best of our way up Channel. When came a little to the west of Folston,[1] Mr. Dawson was put onshore, to go to London in order to fetch the Capt[ns.] wife to him to Dunkerk, and soon after fell in with a fleet of West Indiamen, with sevral cutters and frigats, with their boats out, bring them to to press their men, as at that time there was a little quarrel between the Spanyards and English. We passed through them all with our American coulers set, expecting to be brought to every moment; and as I was the only Englishman onboard, the Capt[n.] advised me to hide myself in the bread locker. But I thought, if they had come on board and found me, I must be gone; so I thought if it was the will of Providence that I should be pressed, let his will be done; and I thought if they should come on board and ask me if I was an Englishman, I should say nothing to the contrary. That if I was stationed on the tops, or anywhere else, God would be with me, and

---

[1] ? Folkestone (see p. 3).

all things should work together for my good. The same day, aboute three or four o'clock, got close in to Calais, where we took a pilot for Dunkerk the same evning, on the 16 September in '90. And as we went up the harbar I saw in a brig's starn, I think, the 'Bettsey, Truro.' I thought if there was any. place caled by that name out of Cornwal, but the next day, as the Captain and I was so great he could then not go onshore without me, nither eate nor drink without me, I was then with him as it were all and in all. It was a great chainge indeed, whether through fear or love I know not. So the next day I, as a complement, asked him to go on board with me to see what the brig was. So it proved to be from Truro, from Petersborg loaden with hemp and iron, there wind bound, and bound to Daniel's Point [1] the first fair wind ; and as I did not want to make myself known unto him as an Englishman, I thought I would let him know that I know sume jentelmen at Falmouth, and after a little discourse sume in Penzance ; so after a while, he naming of one and another until he come home to our family, and added, 'Poor felows, they have had a great many and very great misfortings of late years. Harry, poor felow, lost a valuable lugger, with a valuable cargo, and was obliged to leave his Country, being taken with sume manawar's boat. I saw him in Leghorn, dined and supped with him, and from there he went to America. I have not heard anything

---

[1] On the Fal.

concarning him since ; whether he is dead or alive, I know not, poor felow.' So at laste I said, ' I am the man, and I desire the favour of you to give me a passage home.' He stared like a man frightened, and said, 'I never saw such chainge on any man in my life, and I had no more knoledge of you no more then if I never saw you. Anything in my powar I will gladly do for you. Do you want money, or anything else ? You'l make free with me. I am sorry I cannot take you to sleep with me, as the cabin is full of hemp, etc. Be not afraid of being pressed, as all my men is protected, but you shall not be pressed unless they press me also.' Here I was loste in wonder, love, and praise, seeing how I was presarved the day before from a manofwar, and I looked upon this as if the Lord had worked a merical[1] to send the brig there as if it was on purpose for me.

The Captain used that trade for sume time, but never put into any harbour in France before, but now struck upon a sand bank, and put in there to be repeared, as he had received sume damage, etc. Well, then, I could but only wonder and adore the goodness of God, shorley his paths is in the deep and his ways past finding out. So then I returned again to my little sloop. I staid in Dunkerk eleven days, then sailed for England, arrived at Daniel's Point the 1 Octr. The same night, aboute nine o'clock, arrived home to Kenneggy,[2] to B^r. Charles's.

---

[1] A miracle.   [2] Near Prussia Cove.

So I was received as one rison from the dead, as they know nothing of my coming home, nither had heard from me for aboute twelve months. So after a little I related what cause I had to come, and after I had settled my business I was minding[1] to return to New York again. He said, 'I will send for our brothers in the morning, and praps we may find sumething other wayse.' So earley in the morning they come, and said, 'If you go to America again we shall never see you more ; we think you may stay at home in safety, there is no person will meddle with you, but we advise you first to go aboute this neighberhood as publick as you please, where you are well known, but shun the towns, and after a few days there will no person take notice of you.

I very gladly consented to what they said, this being on Saturday. First went to the King's Cove to see the Cove boys, and for all I was not more than aboute two years from them, not one of them know me until they heard me speak. The next morning being the sabbath, went to Trevean[2] to preaching, where I had a blessed time indeed. After preching I was surounded with allmoste all the congregation. Every one glad to see me, but in particular the methodists, as they heard before that there was a chainge of mind passed upon me. This made me to wonder and adore the goodness of God

---

[1] 'Intending ; dialect.
[2] A small village, about a mile from Prussia Cove.

unto me, as I did not expect to see any person when I came home but only my own family. This was a wonder indeed to think I was once more returned to my native country, amongse my own family, friends, and the people of God. Well, then, after atending the preaching and meetings a few times was desired to give out a hymn and speak in prayer, but at first I refused, as I did not exercise in that way before I come home, only at times I was sent to visit the sick with Father Cooper when he could not atend himself. So I refused, but after suffered great pain of mind, so that at laste I took up the cross with much fear and trembling, and immediately went aboute like a town crier, telling the people what the Lord had done for my soul.

See what a chainge was here taken place; a little while before labouring in the fields with the poor negroes, and used like a slave, and looked upon with contempt on the greatest part of my passage home; so now I had nothing to do with the world, all things was provided for me, so that in a little time the congregation begin to increase greatly, and prayer meetings set on in many defrant places; so, as far as I can remember, in the course of eight or nine weeks there was a great number of men, women, and children converted. Our meeting seem to be all in confusion, sume praying, sume singing, sume crying, sume praising and blessing of God. We have staid in the house sume times from twelve until three o'clock in the morning. My heart at that time, with every powar of my soul, was fully engaged in the work; one time in particular, I trust I shall never for get it, in prayer in the after meeting, I think Mr. Wacktings was the preacher, whether in the body or out of the body I could harely tell. It was just the same as it was in New York, and car'd on in the same manner. At the first sume of the old members would not owned it to be of God, as it was so much out of the comman way, wilst many others put their shoulders to the work, and, praise be to God, aboute this time I do remember my soul through mercy was got just in the same tune as it was in New York. I declard at that time to sevral old members consarning my thoughts. Sume would give me great incoregement, wilst other would try to drive me back. I mentioned this, if ever this should be published, which in all probability it will not, for thou, my young Reader, to take care who to declare thy mind to, for it is not evry old prefessor that knoweth moste of the things of God, but in the genral him who's soul is moste alive to God. So as I was but as a babe in the way, I still wanted to be teached in the ways of God, and I fell in company with John Bettens, to whom I opened my mind freely. I have thought many times since I never found such faith, no, not in all the men I ever talked with. Well, then, I was not confined to Trevean house only, but I went aboute all through the country. But no place where I was asked where

the housen was not full of people, and sume would
not contain all the people. Shorley I was a wonder
to myself, and in genral I found great freedom to
speak to the people in my simple way. I remember
once I went about eight or nine miles from home,
and as I came to the door where I was expected, a
young man came out and said, 'Are you Captain
Harry Carter?' I answered, 'My name is Henry
Carter.' He said, 'We have been expecting of you, for
it is given out for you to preach to-night.' When I
heard of the name preach, I was struck with such
fear and trembling, I could not tell whether it was
best to return home again or stay there. So I went
in, and the good man received me very kindly, and
when the time came took me to the chaple, where it
was so full the people could harley stand. Sume
that know nothing of preaching caled it preaching,
but I never presumed to take a text, but laid a little
foundation as a text in disguise, so that I had room
to ramble. But it was not for what I could say only
that the housen was so full of people, but it was like
the Jews of old, came not to see Jesus only, but
Lazreth [1] also. Where I was not known before, they
heard of me, and they believed that there was a great
chainge upon me. I think the people believed I was
really what I professed to be, but many times after I
had been speaking, so dejected in my own mind,
wishing that I may stand up no more, for it was

[1] Lazarus.

seldam a day passed but what I had doubts whether I was cal'd or not, and I was much afraid to run before I was sent. And likewayse the cross was so great, I have often [1] thought if the people knew what I suffered, they never would ask me to exercise in that way at all. Oh, how I did tremble and sweat just as the time were come. Well, then, still the work of God continued to go on in Trevean society, and lively meetings all through this neighberhood.

I think it was in Febury, in 1791, or a little before, when the work in Trevean begun in sume degree to sease, but still blessed times; and I think it was in the later end of March or the begining of April I was sent for by a great man of this neighberhood, he wanted to speak with me. Accordingly I went, and the business was as follows—saying, 'I was in Helston a such a day in company with three jentelmen' (mentioned their names); 'they all ware black coats. Looking out through the window, a methodist preacher went up street. One said, "There is a methodist prechar." Another answered, "I wonder how Harry Carter goes aboute so publick a preching and Law [2] against him; I wonder how he is not aprended and taken." So I sent for you, as I fear they are brewing of mischief against you.' 'Well, sir,' said I, 'what do you think I am best to do?' He said, 'I know they cannot hurt you no further, then if you are taken

---

[1] Spelt 'oughten' in the manuscript. See note i. p. 5.
[2] Referring to the Government reward for his capture.

you may suffer a long time in prison, and it may cost you a good deal of money, etc. I think you are better, to prevent danger, to return to America again.' This was the tenar of his advice, and added, ' If you go there I will give you, as I *think* he called it, a lett of recome- dation from Lord ——, which, I think, may be very usefull to you, or anything else in my powar shall not be wanting.' And as the jent was well acquainted with our family, I dined with him, and he brought me aboute a mile in my way home, so I parted with him, fully determning in my own mind to soon see my dear friends in New York again. So I told my brothers what the news was, and that I was meaning to take the jent's advice. They answered, ' If you go to America we never shall see you no more. We are meaning to car on a little trade in Roscoff in the brandy and gin way, and if you will go there you'l be as safe there as in America ; likewayse, we shall pay you for your comision, and you car on a little business for your self, if you please.' So that with prayer and supplication I made my request known unto God. I still continued to walk in the same rigrous self *denial as before*, abstaining *from* food, etc. Well, then, with much fear and trembling I concluded to go. The greatest tryal I had aboute going, I know there was no religious people there, and sume times in fears I should be lead away into the world again. I know I was going un slepry ground, but, glory be to God, I know his grace was sufficient for me. So at the 19 of April, in '91, I saild in an open boat from the King's

Cove, in company with a merchant that had business there, so that after fifteen hours' passage arived there very safe, still in the same frame of mind. I lodged at a publick house, I think, two days, and as the merchant had business to Morlaix, desired me to go with him, where I staid there aboute ten or twelve days, and returned again back to Roscoff. I keept myself to myself as much as posable. Well, then, I went to privat lodgings and eate and drunk to myself; and as I had no business to do, I was allmoste all the time to myself day and night, still walking in the same *self deni*al as first. I *would not* allow myself but four hours in bed, so continued, as well as I think, for six or seven days, but I found I had not sleep enough, as aboute noon I have fallen asleep upon the book, so I added a little longer time. I have often times since thought how dead I was then to all below. There was a house burned under the same roof where I lodged little before, and I had to go in and out right before the same house; and after I was there aboute a furtnight I hard sume people talking aboute the dredfull fire, and what great loste sume had sustained. I asked, 'What fire?' They said, 'Next door.' I made no other answer, for I was really ashamed; what they thought of me I know not. So after I looked, and saw moste of the walls standin, but without windows and door, and the walls smoked quite black.

Well, then, I did not pray in secret less than I

F

did before, I suppose never less than ten times in a day, and in fore and afternoon walked a little out of town in so solitary pláce as I could find, out of sight of all men. In genral I went on the cleavs,[1] wher no eye saw me, and there sing, that I may be heard for I suppose a mile distance, and pass, I think, aboute two hours and half fore noon and after noon in reading, praying, singing, and then return home. Aboute this time I made a linen girdle to go aboute my loins inside my shirt. *Tied it* tite —I thought I might be able to live upon *less food* and my sp*irit* would be more vigorous in the wayse of good. I continued on for, as I think, aboute two days, found it quite disagrable, and so left it off. I passed allmoste all my time to myself; in my going out and coming in I went the byest roads, because I wanted to see no person ; and if I meet any person in the way, it was a great cross to me to enter in to any conversation more than just the time of the day, for fear to obstroct my communan with God. I think then I watched over all my thoughts as well as words and acktens.[2] I think there did not the least thought pass my mind unperseved ; my mind then was like a fisherman's net, I sav'd the good but heaved away the bad.

Well, then, I went on still in this way until I think aboute the beginning of August, when I went on with a little business in the shop way, and

---

[1] 'Cliffs'; dialect.   [2] Actions.

aboute the same time Captain B. came there, an old acquaintance of mine, being the first Captain I sailed with, a man of what we calls good morels. I meet him one Sabbath morning as I was walking out, and after a little conversation I said, 'This is a poor place for the publick worship of God; if I was at home now I should be at Trevean preaching.' He answered, 'Why don't you stand up here and say something to the people?' So as I thought he was making game of me, I answered, 'Who will hear me?' He said, 'I will hear you, and I suppose most of the English men in town.' So the next Sabbath morning meet with him again on nearly the same ground. He repeated unto me nearley the same thing again, saying, 'All the English in town will gladly hear you,' or to that purpose. So then I thought he was in earnest, and I left him with much fear and trembling, and immediately went to ask counsel from the mouth of the Lord, so that spent the remainder of that fore noon in pray and supplication, and for fear I should run before I was sent, I set this as a mark, that after diner I would go on the pier, and if I meet first a such a man, who was master of one of the vessels that was there, I should perpose the matter unto him, and if agreable, I should shorly think it to be the will of God consarning me. So aboute one o'clock I roase up from my knees and went on the pier, and the first man I meet with was the very same man, so with much fear and trembling I opened the business unto him of what Captain B. and I was talking of. He readily replyed, ' I'll come, and I will tell all the people of it, I suppose they will all come.' So him and me perposed the time of meeting, I think it was four o'clock. So he, like a town cryar, beat the alarm, and after I left him, oh, how my poor *head was* destracted, a *such* poor *ignorant soul* as I was to take such a thing upon me ; shorley I shall be a by word and reproach with the French, and a mocking and lafing stock to all the English. And another was, what can I say to the people ? as when I was at home there was mornars to comfart, weak belevers to build up, sanctification to impress upon the people's minds, and now only *sinners*, etc., to talk to. So that my poor mind was so full of distraction I could harly tell what to do; but as I had gone so far as to perpose it, I could not go from it. Well, then, according to the time perposed, the same afternoon, in came Captain B. with I suppose aboute twenty or thirty, I suppose nearly all the Inglish men in the town, took off their hats, and seat themselves down, so that I begun to tremble and sweat, I could scarcely hold the hymn book in both hands. Gave out a verse, and begun to sing myself, and praise be to God, before I sung the second verse I found life coming, and before I went to prayer the cross was all gone, so that I found very great liberty in prayer ; so that when I roase from my knees I was surprised to see so many hard harts to their knees, so that I found much curage to go on in my poor simple way. I found uncoman degree of liberty, and the people all listoned with the greatest attention, and after I dismised the people with singing and prayer. So after they were gone, I was still jealous that they would turn what I said into ridicule, and as I had a back window that I could see the greatest part of the pier, watched them, and they all went on board as quiat as Christians of the first magnitude might be expected. The Lord doth only know if there was any good done or not. So I continued for eight or nine months every night when there was Englishmen there. I think it was in the beginning of the month of May '92, when three of my brother's children come to life with me, Fra⁸·, Henry, and Joanna Carter, and staid with me until the beginning of Sept^r·, when I was like a hermit to myself as before. I think it was in the beginning of Oct^r· when three large cuttars, Captain Scott one of them, came in here wind bound from Guarnsey ; and as I went into the house on sume buisiness where they put up to, saw one of their sailors that did formely sail with me. I asked him to come to my house, sayin I could treate him with a glass of grogg, and if them three or four men that was presant would come with him, I should be glad to see them also. This was in the evning. I was not home as I think more than fifteen or twenty minits until he came in with four or five with him, and in a few minits after allmoste the house full with their three Captains. Then I thought what they come for, and as they took me in surprise, as I had not the least thoughts to say anything, I begun to tremble and run upstairs to call for help from the Lord. I suppose I might have been there eight or ten minits, and as I was coming down I meet one in the stairs, saying, ' If you don't come down the people will all be gone.' So with much trembling and sweating I took the Hymn Book and begun to sing to myself, as I did the first time. I found great liberty in prayer, and after thundred out the tretnings, cryed aloude, spar'd not. They all behaved very well, seemed to listen with great atention. So after we concluded the meeting, I asked the Captains and sume of the men to seat down, so they stayed with sume more of their people, I suppose more than an hour, all very seryous, no laffing, no trifling conversation. They took sume thing to drink, shook hands, and wished good night. Prayse be to God, I was shorly a wonder to myself in deed: So the next morning him that had sailed with me before come in laffing, saying one of his shepmates told him that how could that ould man know his thoughts, for he told him allmoste all that ever he did in his life. I think they sailed the next day, and two of them being in company in a gale of wind, one of them disapeared, and have never been heard of since. Captain Scott showed me great kindness ever after ; he sent a luggar there after to be laid up, with, I think, six or eight men on board, who ordered them to take all what they wanted of me, and likewayse recemended all his friends unto me for what they wanted.

Well, then, aboute the later end of Nov^r· I got a passage to come home not only to see my family friends, but my spiritual friends also. I can still see, glory be to God, I was still hungring and thirsting after him. I thought before I come home, if I could be permitted to come into preaching housen dors, I should be very happy, but praise be to God, I had rather the right hand of felowship given me, the preaching houses full of people where I was expected, as before. I staid at home until 24 Dec^r·, and as the war seemed to be near at hand between the Franch and Inglish, inbarked at Coverack, on board Captain R. John's. I had a blessed time in company with my dear freinds there, two or three day wind bound. Arived at Roscoff, Christmas day in the morning.

1 Jan^y· 1793, oh, how short I comes in all things of what I would wish or ought [1] to have been. There was no talk of war when I arived there, all was quiat as when I left the place. I found my house, etc., just as I left it. I was then to myself as before, I went home like a hermat or a king blessing and praising of God. I continued to walk in the same selfdenial. I sent off moste of my goods to Gurnsey, sold sume there, and keept sume, what the law would alow me to bring home, as I was promised that a vessel should be sent to bring me home. So I think Feb^y· 2 [2] there was an embargo lade on all English vessels, and war declard between

---

[1] Spelt 'oft' in the manuscript. See note 1, p. 5.
[2] War was declared on the 1st February 1793.

the boath Kingdoms. I think it was in the latter end of March when I was sent to Morlaix as a prisnor, not close confined, but to apear every morning to the town house to sine my name. I was there nine or ten days, when I was ordered back to Roscoff again. Things at that time looked very gloomey, but glory be to God, I was not the lease afraid of all the lyons in France. I could trust boath soul and body in the hands of my Redemer, no mormring, no complaining, the language of my heart was continualy, 'Good is the will of the Lord, may thy will be done.' I staid in Roscoff nine or ten days, when I was ordered again to Morlaix in company with Mr. and Mrs. *McCullock* and Mr. *Clansie*. I think in the beginning of May was sent back again to Roscoff, Mr. M. and Mr. C. in Roscoff the same time, where we was all obliged to go to the town house every day to sine our names. So continued untel the beginning of August, when we got a passport in order to come home. In the course of this time, wilst in Morlaix, the same as at Roscoff, went to privat lodgings. Walking still in the same rigrous selfdenial, etc. So as there was no other way for us to come home, M. Macculloh bought a small vessel, aboute 40 tons, and boute the seven or eight hauled the vessel out in the Sadle Rock Road, and got all things on board ready for sea, when there was orders from the town house with a corvet's armed boat, ordered us in to the pier again. And this was Provedence indeed.

Our whole crew consist as follows : Mr. Macculloh was a jentleman marchant, lived in that town many years before, a man of good property, etc.; Mrs. Macculloh, two sons, one a man, the other aboute twelve years old, one daughter, a young lady aboute eighteen or twenty years old, one sarvant man, two sarvant maidens, Mr. Clansice, and myself, ten in number in all. And we concluded before, that the old jentleman and me was all the sailors, there was not one of the other eight that in no case could help themselves. The four females was sent onshore to Mr. M.'s house, all the rest of us keept on board with a gard of soldars for three days and three nights, the wind blowing very hard tho' fair. This vessel was condemed for sea for sume time before, so that in the cource of three days we had time to over-haul her, and I think I may safely say that there was scores of graving pieces in her not bigger then a man's hand ; sume of the timbrs so rotton, that one might pick them off with one's fingers, the sails, masts, etc., in the like state. We had hard rain sume part of that three days, where we was so wett below nearley as upon deck. The old jentleman have told me many times since, saying it was Providence prevented us from sailing, had we sailed then we should all be no more. You may be ready to ask, Why did we expose ourselves to so much dainger? I answer, 'This was the third pasport, and all conterdicted, and glad to git out of the mouths of the lyons, as there was no other way.' So we was all sent on shore to Mr. M.'s house with a gard of soldars to be keept at the dore, and the 15 of August, 1793, all march'd to St. Paul's with a gard of soldars. I lodged and boarded in the house with Mr. and Mrs. M., where I had a good room and bed to sleep in, and a large garden to walk in. Now, I am going to inform you of sume of the devices of Satan. One evning, whilst at suppar, seating by the side of Mr. M., when it was sugested to my mind the same as if *one* was to speak to my outward ear blasfamys thoughts against my dear friend Mr. M. At first it struck me all of alarm. Upon reflection I was shore they were not my thoughts, for at that time, and before then, I know I never loved my own father bettar, and after, when the gulenteen[1] begun to work, I have thought many a times, should him be condemned, I would gladely die in his steed. So after suppar took a walk in the gardon as usual, where I begun to reason, saying, 'Shorley if I was saved from inbred sin, I should not feel such ugley thoughts as these and then begin to doubt.' But praise be unto God, he did not leve me to doubt for harley a moment, but sent me down the Comfartar, so that all doubts vanished away in a moment. So I went to seat in the summar house, and begun to sing, that I suppose that I might be heard all over the town. I suppose I shall never forgett that evning wilst in time, how my poor *soul* was delighted

---

[1] Guillotine.

in God my Saviour. Still went on in the same
rigrous selfdenial, but I could not fast then for
fear to be taken notice of with the family. I staid
there until the 12 or 13 September, 1793, when sume
officers came, sent by the town house ; so after they
examined us for money and papars, took us to the
Town House, and after they measured our height,
and asked us many foolish questions, took us to a
prison caled the ' Retreat,' in the same town. We
arived there a little after night, were all of us showed
our apartment to lodge in. I had a nice little room
to myself like a king. Here was another chainge,
but a happy one, the language of my heart was,
' Good is the will of the Lord, may Thy will be done.'
Nor could I help singing that night alowd when I
went into bed. We all had our pervision sent from
the House we lodged before, and after four or five
days past, we was joined by sevral French gent. and
lades, and in aboute fourteen or fifteen days there
was two armed horsmen sent in the preson to take
Mr. and Mrs. M. from us, no person knowing where
they were to be sent, but supposed they were to be
sent to a small uninhabited island, a little off Brest
harbar, and there to be starved to death. Oh, what
tears and cries was there with their little famely and
many others. It was seldom I could shed tears, then
I did plenty, and after dried up my tears and cheard
myself up, and then went in to his room, where I found
him alone packing up his clothes, etc. I sat myself

down in silence I suppose for aboute ten minutes with out one word ; whether him or me spoak first, I know not, but he said in his usual plesant way to this purpas, ' I fear not what man can do unto me. I can trust in Providence and not be afraid,' which set my heart all on fire with love ; I could give them both up unto God, shorley beleving I should see them again. The remainder of the day was a solam day unto me in deed, but a day of mourning through the whole house ; after this there did seldam a day pass but what sume Jentmen and Ladis was brought to join us, and in the beginning of Nov. 1793 the lady I boarded with and sume of her famely was brought to us. I used sett times for reading, praying, walking, and thinking, as I did before when I was at liberty, and keept allmoste all the time to myself; I went to bed aboute ten or half past, and got up as soon as I could see daylight in the morning ; and as the weather begun to alter, juste to run in the garden aboute half hour in the fore noon, and the same in the after noon. At first the people thought I was ither a natural fool or else mad, but my friend Clansie gave them an account of what kind of being I was. Aboute this time I had word brought me, that all my goods *I left* in Roscoff was condemed and sold, I suppose they might have been to the amount of £40. I rejoiced with great joy when I heard of it, saying the Lord's will be done, knowing all things should work twogether for good. It apears clearley to me since that my will was wholy swallowed up in the will of God ; I think I was then shorley so dead to this world as ever I shall be. Well, then, as the people begin to increase more and more evry day, Mr. Clansice came with me in my little room. At first it was a great cross to me, but soon after, the oftener I saw him the better, far bettar I likt him, he ackted like a father, a brother, my tuter, my sarvant. Glory be to God for such dear frends. He was a young jentelman merchant, a man of great natural abilities, and I suppose brought up in the first scools in Christendom. I knew his father and him from a child before, but was little acquainted with him before we became prisonars together, and I have thought many times since that there was not in the whole world two such men as Mr. M. and he. Aboute the 3 or 4 of Decr 1793 a gard of soldars came into the prison and took with them my dear friend C., Mr. T. Maccull, with a great number of French gintelemen and ladis, so there was none of my family left, but Miss M., her dear little brother, and the two sarvant maidens. I think such a scene as that I never saw in all my life. I suppose there was not one dry face in all the house, *either* with men or whimin. There was not one *person* that know where they were to be sent to, but supposed they were all to be sent upon the same Island with Mr. and Mrs. M., and there to be starved to death. This was a day of mourning and lamentation indeed. I do not know that I shed one tear, tho' it was a solamn day with me, still the language of my heart was, 'Good is the will of the Lord, may the Lord's will be done.' But the tryal was so great, the same as tearing the flesh from the bones.

Aboute the 6 Decr. 1793, when a gard of soldars came to the preson, and took away I suppose between thirty and forty prisnors, and me one of them, where to go we knew not; but Provedence enterfered, and worked upon a French jintelman's mind, so that he took Miss Maccu^h. and her little brother, with the two maidens, to his own house, so that they had all liberty to walk the town when they pleased. This was the cause of great joy and gladness unto me. There was a few horses brought for the old and infarm to ride— two, which one was put in my hands, and ordered to ride it, with a charge to keep it to myself. We had aboute twelve French miles to go, so we arived to Morlaex just after night, where, to my agreable surprise, found dear C., Mr. T. M., and sume jint^n. of Roscow, whome I know before. We rejoiced greately together, and then they *gave* an acount of Mr. and Mrs. Maccu^h.; they was put *from* St. Paul's to a town caled Landernau, aboute twenty miles from S^t. Paul's, in to a crimnal gaol, where the first night had nothing to lye on but a little short dirty straw, and without one farding ¹ of money with them, and not one person in the town that they were acquainted with, but in the morning was visited with sume jint^n. and lades, who

---

¹ 'Farthing'; dialect.

suplyed them with a bed, and brought them pervisian.
So we rejoiced greatly together in telling and hearing. Here was a blessed chainge again to me, to
once more to be with my dear family at home again.
This place we was now in was a jentelman's house,
all the family thrust out and put into other prisons,
and this house made a prison of. The house was not
large, but it was full of people below and aloft. I
sleept in one room, where there was fourteen beds,
and there could not find the least cornar to retire to
myself but a little house. At that time it was very
cold, but I did not mind that. I could not stay there
long to a time, distorbed with one or other, as there
was sixty or seventy presoners there. I had not one
farding of money, nor nither of our family, but the
law or rule was, by the order of the Convention, for
the rich to maintain the poor. So I think I was
maintained by the publick for two days, when my
friend C. got credit for himself and me, from a
tavarn close by. What a great chainge this was
again, all the day long in nothing but a discord
and noise. What a mercy it was I was not *draw*ed
away by the multitude to do evil. I can see now at
this moment how I improved my time, how prechas
every moment was, I had allwayse my book in my
pocket ready to hand if I could find any place to
seat, and sume times, when I could find no place to
seat, stand to read. All the people very civil to me,
and in the beginning many of them introduced their

conversation; but I did not find it profatable, it sarved to block the mind from prayer. Tho' I could understand and speak French on moste common subjects, I soon gave them to think I know little or nothing, so by that means I saved myself from a great deal of empty chatchat, so by that means pass allmoste whole days, sume times without speaking very little. I have often heard sume of the French gentlemen speaking very high thing in my favour one to another, not knowing I could understand them, and I think it had allwayse this efect to humble me as in to the dust before God and before man. I was still watching over all my thoughts with all my words and actions. I do realy now beleve that there did not one thought pass through my mind unperseved in all my waking moments, still living as under the immediate eye of God, walking in the broad light of his countanance from moment to moment. I had left of drinking of water from the year of '89 in America, but there was a well close by the backdoor. I had *a* tumblar glass where I went sume times, and *filled a* glass with water, and look at it again and again. Oh, how my heart would burn with love and thankfulness to God. Aboute a week after I was there, I had a book given me by a French gent. that spoak English, caled 'The Sinner's Guide,' pen'd by a Spanyard, but translated in English. The name of the gent· that gave it me was Mr. Lereu, which proved a great blessing to me indeed.

25 Dec^r·, or Christmas day, 1793, Mr. T. M. and Mr. S. was taken from us, and put to a town caled Carhay,[1] aboute thirty miles from Morlaix, and there they joined Mr. and Mrs. Maccu^h·; all the rest of us was moved to another Jen^t· house, a few dors off, where we had more room, etc., Mr. C. and me still left together. The first thing I allwayse lookt for first was a place to go in secret, and my friend C. would allwayse look out for a place for himself and me to sleep in. I found a nice *little* place in the garat, with sume old mats and other things I so inclosed, that it would just hold me to my knees, with my feet out of sight, where I might stay so long as I pleased, and no person distorb me. This was a blessed chainge again. I sleept in a room with ten or twelve gent^m·, went to bed at ten o'clock, got up in the morning at five, *spent an* hour to myself, and at six went down stairs, *and sat by* the fire with the old men that garded *the hous*e. To read, etc., until aboute half past seven or eight, when I should retire to my little garat until nine, when I should come down, make my bed, and run or walk in a large room until ten, and then retire again to my garat until one o'clock, when I was caled to dinnar. After dinnar, aboute two, I retired to my garat and stay there until half past three, come down and run in the room until four, then retire, and stay there until aboute seven or eight, stay down aboute half hour, and then pass in the

[1] Carhaix.

garat until ten, bed time.   There was a small window
in the garat aboute a foot square, without glass, but
a leef to shut and open, so that in the daytime could
see to read by it, but at night I seat without any
light, the days nearley the same length as they are
in England.   At that time I begun to, what I call,
to examen myself, which time was from half past six
until aboute nearley eight in the evning—about the
same time that the many thousands of methodists
offered up their evning sacrifise in England—and
begin first to see the many wonderfull delivrances
the Lord had wrought for me—how I have been
presarved so many times from drowning and other
dangars, then how I was convinced of sin, how I
cal'd for mercy, what tryals and temptations when I
was seeking the Lord, how and when I receved the
Comfarter, what tryals, temptations, when I was in a
justified state, what   , what fears, what joys
and delights in all plases I have   since I know the
goodness of God ; how many times I prayed in secret
in evry place, what self denial I walked in, and to
conclude, sume up the whole, saying, ' Lord, how is it
with me now ; am I growing in grace or loosing of
ground?'   This garat was very cold indeed to the
body, so that my hands was swollen very large with
chilblins, sitting so many hours in the cold without
fire.

Jan^y· 1794, aboute the beginning of the year,
Mr. C. got me to sleep with him in his little room

and one French jen[t]. This was again a comfartable chainge; there we was together again, like to great *kings*. Aboute the latar end of this month, I was desired by C. to speak to aboute twenty whemen caled nuns, being presnars in the same house. I went with fear and trembling. They received me in a very *pleasant* manner, drew a chear,[1] asked me to seat down. *One of them, an* old lady, the mother Confessor, asked *me, was* I ever baptised. I answered, 'Yes.' 'In what manner?' I answered, 'I was marked with the sign of the Cross in the name of the Father, and of the Son, and of the Holy Gost.' I saw sume thing very plasant upon all their countnance, as it was the same way they themselvs was baptised. They asked me a number of many fullish questions, that I was obliged to mustar all the little French I could rise, as I could understand and speak any thing aboute the coman things of this life far better than the spiritual things, having no person to converce with aboute spiritual things. However, they keept me with them I suppose aboute half hour, still asking me questions, but at laste asked me to kiss the Cross. I refused. They tried me again and again. I told them I could not, I dare not do it. So at laste took my leave of them, and so came off rejoicing like a king. They are a loving people, and the nicest whemen I ever saw in France. I doubt not but many of them lives accord-

---

[1] 'Chair'; dialect.

ing to the light that is given them. They petted me
very much, and told my friend afterward that if he
could prevail upon me to turn to their Religion, I
should be a good man. They thought I was earnestly
crying for mercy, but was an entire strainger to the
way of mercy. They allwayse looked upon me afterward with the love of pity, *and some* of them was
fond to converse with me,   found
it profitable, they after caled   the
soletude, I spent so much time to myself. I think it
was the 11 or 12 of Feb^y· '94, I seat apart to prayer
and fasting on a particular occasion for thirty hours
without eating or drinking. At the 19 and 20 of the
same month, I seat apart in prayer and fasting to
ask of the Lord sevral favours for self and friends,
with thanks for past mercys, forty-eight hours without eating or drinking. Oh, what a blessed time I had.
The 19 and 20 of April, 1794, I seat apart in prayer
and fasting for forty-eight hours without eating or
drinking. I trust I shall ever remember these times
wilst I am in time. Oh, how my poor soul was
delighted in God my Saviour. To the end of this
time I went to run in the room as usual, willing to
know whether I was weaker or not, so that I found I
could run as strong as ever I could ; and it was shorley
to me *a great* wonder, as I took no breakfast for
aboute six months *before* then, and I took suppar sume
times two, and sume times *three times* a week, and
my suppar I suppose did not exceed two ounces of

bread, without tea, water, or anything to drink, and my dinnar very little. I was still suplied with dinnar from the tavern. Mr. C., and aboute six or eight French gen^{t}, dined together. I could not keep all this a secret from my friend, so he took me to reason sevral times, saying, 'You'll destroy the body,' and would intice me like a child to eate, and allways took the pains to call me to dinnar. So *I thought* it was reason what he said, and I thought I was *going to* too great extremes, so I thought for the time to *come I would* go without breakfast and suppar as usual, *and fast* for thirty hours once month, for the time to come. I did not know then at that time I was thankfull or humble, but even now, I know I was as less then nothing in the sight of God and all men. I know I was unworthy of the floor I walked on, and vilest of the vile in my own eyes. I never saw my short comings more clearer than I did in them days. Oh, how often I was crying out against my dryness and lasiness of soul, my littleness of love, etc. Sume times, when I heard the clock strike, I uste to rejoice, saying, 'Lord, one hour nearer to Eternety,' the same time mourn before God I did not spend it more to his glory. I think every moment of time was far more preshas then fine gold. Aboute this time there was numbers of gen^{t} and lades *taken* away to Brest that I parsnally know, and their *heads* chopt off with the gulenteen [1] with a very little notice. I don't

---

[1] Guillotine.

know I ever had a doubt of my own life, but I have had many of Mr. M., and thought many times, should he be condemed to die, I would gladly die in his steed if Providence would have it.   I knew he had much enimies, and why, because he was a libral man and a man of powar, and did do much good, and them he did do most good to was his greatest enimyes, and it was *such men* as him in genral suffered moste. Ag*ain*   if he was spared, he was worth his *place in* creation, be helpful to others as well as his own famely.   As for me, ī thought I should never be found wanting with any person in the world.   I know my child at home would be taken care of, so it was a mattar of very little defrance to me where the body was left, knowing I had a house not made with hands, eternal in the Heavens.   I staid there until the 15 June, 1794, when the house was cleared of all the presnors, and then put to a convent a little out of Town, that was made a prison, caled the Calemaleets,[1] where there was aboute 270 men and whimen, the house very full of people.   We arived there aboute nine in the morning, and as Mr. C. and me was shifting aboute the house seeing for a place, standing in the *room* talking together, he was taken with a fit and fell *as* dead in my arms.   Soon others came to my asistance, *and took* him out in the yard as dead. It was very seldem *that I* shed tears, but then I did plentefully, as I was in m*ind* he was no more ; but the

---

[1] ? Carmelites.

language of my heart was *still*   *may* thy
will be done ; come life or death, take life *and all*
away, good is the will of the Lord.   But praised *be
the Lord for* ever, in the course of an hour he revived,
and *was put to* bed, so that in the course of sume
time after *he recovered.*   In the garden I seat myself
under a tree and *thought of H*agar's words, 'Thou, God,
seest me.' I had a sweet time there until *I was disturbed*
by two young *men* that came to seat by *me*
with a great m*errime*nt and ladies, and *soon after* the
Lord provided a place for me under the stairs.   It
was a large stone stairs going down to a underground seller.   In the daytime I could see a small
glimring light, but never so light as to see to read.
This was a blessed place again, indeed, where I was
out of sight and hearing of all men.   Mr. C. got
part of a room in the garat, with a young jen*t*, whose
name was Morrow.   The first night I made my bed
in the passage close by his door.   Friend C. could not
bear to see me there.   The next morning him, with
sume young jen*t*, got carpentar's tools and timber,
turned to and divided the room in two, so took me
in with him again, and there we was again together
like two great kings.   We could no longer have our
food from the tavarn, the distance being too far
The good lady that I lodged and boarded with in St.
Paul's was brought to the same preson, and a young
gentleman with her, her brother son, to which she
had dear C. and me with her to eate.   She had her

per*vision* sent from her own house. Blessed be God for such dear Friends. In the course of two *or three* days I found my strength much failed me. *I had* more room to walk in than I had before, *and* long *stairs* to go up and down over. Mr. C. *discovered* it, and took me again to reason, saying, ' *You are* of the earth, and the body must be *helped with thing*s of the earth ; if you continue so, you'll *hurt yourself*, and if you do not *feel* any ill efects *now   you* shorley will if *you* lives untel you are old.' I thought it was quite reason that he preached to me. I thought I was going too far with it, and that Satan had some hand in it ; so after he watched me like a child, and if I was not presant at the time of meals, he would come and fetch me, and I must go with him, he would not be denied. Praise be to God that I ever saw his face, he was allwayse more mind-full of me than he was of himself ; so I continued to take breakfast for eight or nine days and then left it off again, and I unely staid without suppar twice a week. This place was again a blessed chainge in deed. We had a large garden to walk in, from six in the morning untel seven in the evning, I suppose not less than three acres of ground, with fine gravel walks in it and sume apple trees, etc., so I was like a bird left out of a cage. I suppose I had not sung aloud to be heard with [1] man for many months before. *I was* allways surounded with [1] man, but then I

---

[1] Meaning ' by ' ; dialect.

used to go out with my book in my pocket, seat mys*elf under* a tree, and if I could not see any person, sing *so loud*, I suppose I might be heard for a mile off. Oh, *how my* soul would be delighted in the God of my sa*lvation*. I remember one day, as I was seating under *a tree*, three or four ladies came to me, and asked me *to sing*. *I begged* to be excused. They asked me again and again, so *as I was afraid* to give an ofence I sung two or three versis *with* a loud voice. They thanked me in a very p*leasant manner*, and went away quite pleased. I think I spent my time *to myself much* the same as I did in Roscoff, before *I was taken* as a presonar. *I was* allwayse mindfull of my little cornar under the stears. I went to bed at ten o'clock, and got up in the morning at four. All the people still full of friendship to me ; but I keept myself still to myself as much as posable, without giving an ofence. There was there amongst the whole number aboute sixty nuns, one of whom I conversed with more then all the rest ; seldom miss a day, if she saw me, but what she would have sume thing to say unto me. But I had not French enough to enter into any depth of Religion, but I never heard one sound of persuasion from her to turn to her Religion. Once I remembered she asked me, saying, 'Carter, did not you feel your self very sorry when you was first convinced of sin ?' or sume thing to the same purpas. I was struck with wondar where she got that from. I think I may

safely say she was a burning and a shining light.
She had small suplys often from *her*   *fat*her's
house, and well she had it often as it was *possible.*   *It
was al*wayse in her powar to govern her own mind.
Every day she would give allmoste all she had to the
poor, *or to any* person she thought that wanted ; lived
allmoste *entirely on* bread and water herself. She have
often told friend *C.,* ' Do not leave Carter want any
thing, but speak *to me.'*   I have often thought that
she would allmoste *tear out* her eyes to do me good,
and I have often thought *that she ha*d not the least
doubt but what I was built *for a Catholi*ck.   I have
thought then, the same as I think *now, that if I* am
faithfull untel death, and she cont*inued in the sa*me
way, that she and me, with many *more that* I saw
there, shall meet at God's right hand, where we shall
sing louder and sweeter that ever I sung in that
gardon.   May the Lord grant it.   She was so nice,
butifull a young lady as I think the sun could shine
on ; I suppose aboute 26 or 27 years old.   Her
father was a nobleman of a large income, her mother,
a sistar to the great, rich Bishop of St. Paul's, and him,
as I have heard, for all his incom, could scarsely keep
a goode sute of clothes aboute him—it was busy all [1]
for the poor.   I think she was the pictar of humility
in all her deportment.   I could not help to admire

---

[1] A common expression in West Cornwall.   It is a forcible way of
saying that his means were fully occupied.

her, as I was in the same house, or housas, for, as I think, nearly six months.

Well, then, I continued to go on in the same manner as did before, minding the same things, and using the same language as I did in every chainge or place; this is the right place that God *would* have me be in, without one mormoring *thought*, or the leaste desire to be anywhere else, *good* is the will of the Lord, happy still from *moment* to moment. It was aboute the later end   it was imprest upon my mind to make   , as there was sume country men there tha*t was doing* it, and after, with prayer and suplication, *I made my* request known unto God, I begun to wo*rk*. *I went* to bed still at ten, roase at three in the *morning, at* four went to work until nine, pass a h*our in prayer under* the stairs, work until half past eleven, *and then dinner*; after dinner pass a half hour u*nder the stairs*, and work untel four, pass a half h*our again in prayer*, work until half past six; at seven *we had supper*. The remainder of the evning spend in praying, walking, reading, thinking, etc. So as the days shortend I could read but very little, nither walk in the garden, but only on the Lord's day. But praise be unto God, he was ever with me in a powarfull manner, sume times when the walks was allmoste full of jent. and lades, pass through them all, as if allmoste there was no soul there but God and me only. That gardon was as the gardon of Edon to my soul.

Then, in the morning, I spent nearly one hour to my-self, and gitt at work as soon as I could see, minding the same stops under the stairs, and work as *long as* I could see in the evning.   So as the weather *got* coulder, I got myself to work in a large *room*, I suppose not less than 50 feet one way, and *I suppose* aboute 30 the other ; it was not finished, *neither plastard* nor floored ; what was under foot was *the ground*, the top of the window just to the level of *the roof* ; and after suppar, evry evning, I passed my *time there* until bed time.   I had a stool to seat un at *meals*, and in the evnings seat on my stool, then *to* pray, etc. ; sume times, without [1] it was *moonlight*, *stum*ble up again [2] the walls, as I had *no light* ; *but* praise be to God for ever, for all it was so cold, a solatry place, it was a paradice to my soul, it was sume thing like a hermitage indeed. I was out of sight and hearing of all men and things.   So just aboute that the clock struck ten, my dear friend C. and me used to meet just at the same time in our little dark cornar of our lodging room as cheerfull as two kings.   I think it was in the medle of Dec^r· 1794, the good ladey and her brother's son was removed from us and put to St. Paul's, into the prison that I was first put in.   It was a day of mourning and lamen-tation with her, indeed, to leave her two children behind her, and it was a time of tryal to me like-wayse, as she was nearly so natural as a mother.

---

[1] Meaning 'unless' ; dialect.   [2] Meaning 'against' ; dialect.

But still the language of my heart was as usual—good is the will of the Lord. She *took* care to send us our provisan from her *own* house, so still dear C. and me was together li*ke* . Aboute this time I had an account that Mr. and Mrs. *Maccullock* was labrated out of preson,[1] and they and all their *family were* then at Mr. Diot's, in Morlaix. It was a day of rejoicing *to* me, indeed, to think that the Lord was so graciou*s to bring* us so near together again. And in the course *of a few* weeks they had liberty to come to see dear C. and *me in prison. We* shorley had a happy meeting together, as w*e had not seen* each other for aboute fifteen months ; they receved *me as their* own child, and I them as my father and mother. *Praise God* for so many dear friends.

Aboute the 10 *Jan*ʸ· 1795, Mr. Diot *sent for* me to come to dine with him. I went with much fear and trembling, as it was ever a great cross to me to be with my great superiers, and so in every place I moved at a solam awe of the presance of God resting upon me with a fear to ofend him. There I meet with Mr. and Mrs. M., with all their loving famely, and through the tender mercy of God, after all our tryals and sufferings, being separated to nearley sixteen

---

[1] Robespierre was executed on 28th July, 1794. Soon after his death the Convention decreed that ' Prisoners and other persons under accusation should have a right to demand some " Writ of accusation," and see clearly what they were accused of.'—Carlyle : *French Revolution*, Book vii. ch. i. This decree was followed by the release of great numbers of ' Suspect ' and other prisoners.

months from each other, escaped, through mercy, all the lyons in France, not one hair of our heads diminished. We staid there until evning, when Mr. Diot said, 'I will in the course of a few days gitt you out of preson and you shall boath come to live at my house.' We thanked him, wished good night, and arived at home with our gard aboute seven. So the 23 Jany. 1795, in the morning, we was boath librated. I went to Mr. Diot's, Mr. C. went with Mr. Morrow in the same town. Still pervision at that time *very* scarce to be had, the inhabitants of the town had all their *provisions* sarved out every day according to their famely. *Without* we had money we should not be able to gett board *on any* account. I was received *into t*hat famely as a king, treated as if I had been a noble-*man*, *and* being the laste strainger was placed at the head of *the table*, where I begged to be excused again and again, but *could not* prevail. But to the end of six or seven days I shifted *to the other* end, where I thought I was more in my place. *I thought* it then, as I have many times since, a piece of *bread be*hind the kitchen door was more suitable for me. *Praise be* to God, here was a chainge again indeed. *From* a stable to a parlar, and from a parlar to a   . *I eat* mostimes my three meals, *then* for fear to be not*iced, I always eat* sparingly. I think I can say I allwayse *rose up with a* sharper apetite then I had when I sat down. I lodged in a large house to myself next dore to Mr. Diot's, where I had no person to desturb me day nor night. This was a blessed chainge again, it was just the place I would wish to be in. I was there aboute two or three weeks, when I saw sume things wanting to be done aboute two vessels that was laid up before my door, belonging to Mr. Diot. I spoak of it to Mr. Peter Diot, and went to work, and when the season sarved, I washed the decks morning and evening ; and as I had a chest of carpentar's tools in the same room with me, made boats' oars, ruddars, painted names in the starn of the small boats, etc. ; that I was mostly imployed all the week. But my wark not hard, as I was my own master, and I did it all volentary. And on the Sabbath day I went out of town evry morning and afternoon when the weather was *fair* in sume solatry place to read, pray, sing, and *think*, as I did in other places. I think it was aboute *the* midle of March 1795, Mr. M. was taken sick with *fever* and agas, and in the beginning of May 1795 went *away* with all his famely, leaving only the two ma*idens and* me behind him. It was the 10 or 12 of Ju*ne that* I went to S*t.* Paul's and Roscoff to see my old f*riends, where* I was received like a king, and with [1] sum*e people* I never had but very little acquaintance *with*. *I had* my time to my-self as usual, only at   meals. I found the same solatry plac*e as before*, where I was brought to examine *myself* whether I was growing in grace or *not*   so I had a bl*essed time*. I returned back

---

[1] Meaning 'by' ; dialect.

again to Morlaix aboute the 26 or 27 June, 1795, like a jiant refreshed with new wine. There I was received again with that loving family with the greatest afection. Praise be unto God for so many dear friends. It was nearley aboute this time I went with aboute a half a score men to put a boat of Mr. Diot's in a large building that was before a tobacko manefactry in the shade, and after I had got the boat to the place I wanted, I went from the people to gett a cornar to myself to pray, and looking aboute I saw a large scales and weights close by me. I thought as no person saw me I would way myself, and all the weight my weight was 6 score and 15 pound.[1] I was set to *won*der where all my weight was gone, as I did for *many* years before way 10 score, and when I came *home* I tried un a waistcoat that I had not worn for *several* years before, and I found it too big for me, *may* be upon the round nine inches, and I never know in all these years no not *one single day* of sickness. I think it was the 10 July, 1795, Capt[n.]   *the* Capt[n.] of a frigat that was taken, and Mr. Moress   *of* the 'Elazander' man-of-war, came *to Morlaix in* order to gett a passage to England in a *vessel*, who dined and supped at Mr. Diot's. *They* made very free with me all *the same as if I* was their equal, and one day, by a friend, desired me to call at their lodging, they

[1] The Cornish people always measure weight in scores (20 lbs.). The stcne (14 lbs.) is unknown.

wanted to speak with me. I went with fear and trembling, and the business was as follows. They said, 'Mr. C., we have been talking about you, as you have been here so long a prisnor, wearing your old clothes out, your time passing away, earning nothing. We think you may go with us in safety. Put your clothes on board the evning before we sail, gett on board in the night, you'l never be inquired after, nither found wanting.' I answerd to this purpas: 'Jen^{t}, I thank you kindly, but first you'l give me leave to inform you I was brought out of prison upon Mr. Diot's interest, tho' he never sined any paper, nither gave his word that I should continue in the country. Notwithstanding that, in these critical times, if I was to go without his leave, he might be caled to an account for it after ward. If you will be so good as to ask Mr. Diot, and with his leave, I will gladly go with you.' They commended me very much, and said *the* first opertunity they would ask him, and I should know of them again. In the course of two or three days *I* waited on them again. Mr. Morress said to m*e*, '*Well*, Mr. C., we have opend your case to Mr. Diot. Mrs.   , him long with you ; he is a great fool to sto*p here* so long as he have, I wounder how he have *not gone* long before now. But Mr. D. said you was *best to* stay a little longer,' and added, 'Mr. C., providen*ce has* presarved and provided for you in a mer*ciful manner,* so I would advise you to waite with *patience, and you*

H

will be deliverd in God's due time.' I th*anked them and* took my *leave of* them, wondring w*here that* should come from, for it was th*e words of a spiri*tual man. I went in one of my solatry cornars and there sung, and blessed and praised God. I can allmoste feel at this moment how happy and thankfull I was, so well and contented equaly to stay as to go ; and if it was the will of God, I should stay there all my lifetime, still, good is the will of the Lord, may His will be done.

So I continued to my work aboute the boats and vessels as before, walking in the same self-denial, until the 6 or 7 of August, 1795, when, unexpected, on Saturday received a letter from Mr. M——h to meet him at S^t. Paul's next Monday, that he had obtained a pasport for himself, famely, and me to go to England, and Mr. Clansee was then at Brest, who had then got a nutral ship to take us home. Well, then, *this* was a great as well as unexpected news, and many *times* before then thought that I should be very glad and thank*ful* if I ever lived to see such chainge. But it answered the same efect as every other change I passed through, a fear I should meet with anything that should obstruct my communan with the Lord, and this is my mening when you read of any case before, when I said I went in fear and trembling. So that on Monday mor*ning I set out* for S^t. Paul's *in* C°. with Mrs. Diot and her two little *children and t*wo sarvants riding in a coach, and me

on horseback, where we arived at S^t. Paul's at ten in
the morning, and there joind Mr. and Mrs. M. and
their loving famely.   Staid there untel Tuesday
morning with my dear old friend and Mother, Madam
Esel le Pleary, and set out for Landernau in company
with the two maidens.   We arived at Landernau
aboute three in the after noon.   Wensday morning
breakfast with my two old friends, Mr. and Mad^m·
Elel Renard, and old jen^t. and young lady, who was
his daughter.   We was many months prisonars
togither, but then all librated, and they in their own
house.   Same morning took a boat, and at four in the
afternoon arived on board the ship *in* Brest harbar,
where we met all the fam*ily* together, the same
ten of us that was stop*ped to*gether through a merical
of mercy in d*eed, and* not one hair of our heads
diminished.   *Praise be* to God, here was another
chainge.   This ship was form*erly an Engl*ish frigate,
then under Danish coulars, *and* the Captn· an English
man.   The *first night* I sleept on the cabin flooar
covered *with a* great coat, then got a hammack
        amongst the sailors.   And when mor*e people
came* on board, I went between decks, being
more quiat.   I suppose the whole numbar of pa-
sengars was aboute fifty offesars in the army and
navy, where I never was in such hurry and noise
yet, in all the course of my life, nither to sea nor
land.   I was allwayse imploid in reading, in cooking,
tending my famely to the table, etc.   And there was

a black boy, the sarvant to one of the officers, very ill moste of the time, and no person to do the leaste thing for him but myself onely.   I had a quiat place between decks to lodge in and pray, so that no person desturbed me.   I used the same self-denial as before.   I have been often led to wonder many times since of the goodness of God, for all they *were* such wild, distracted, disapated souls, I never *had the* least tryal from one of them, nither one *of the* ship's company during the whole time.   I could *always* bring any dish of meat from the cook to the *cabin to* my famely, and no person set the least hand *on me* ; *or* if one of the others did, they was ready allmoste *to kill* one the other ; and the Captain would trust me *with the* tea and shugar canestar, but not one person *else* on board.   I have thought many times *since aboute* it, more than at that time through   d favour with God and man.   *We lay in Brest* Roade nine days *wind* bound, and then *got a fair* wind to the Nor*thwa*rd and westward   etc., arived at Falmouth 22 August, 1795.   Arived onshore aboute three o'clock in the afternoon with much fear and trembling, where I meet with my dear little Bettsy, there staying with her aunt, Mrs. Smythe, then between 8 and 9 years old.   In the evning went to prayer meeting in the great Chaple. I said sumething to the people, but found but little liberty.   I thought the cause might have been after aboute three weeks exposed to so much noise and company, and for want of composure of mind, and likewayse so long a time out of the habit of exercising in that way. I have thought many times since, if I was ever dead to the world and to myself, I was then in them days. It matterd but little where my lott was cast, whether in prosperity or adversity, whether sickness or health, take life or all my friends away, I could trust boath soul and body, with every thing *that* I had, in to the hands of my great Creator with*out the* leaste resarve. I have thought many times since *in them* days, tho' I did not know it then, that I had no will, or rather, of my own, but my will w*as* loste in the will of God. It is now brought *into my* remembrance as the ship lyed to off *Falmouth* harbar, there was not boats enuf to *carry all the* pasangers and bagage at once, and I *waited to* the laste with two more, staid untel *another* boat should come, the wind blowing *fresh from* the westward. The Captain grew v*ery impatient, looking* out for a boat, and at laste said, ' *I shall not wait* only a few minuts longer, and ta*ke you with me.*' One of these p*asangers was m*aking *such a* noise, allmoste ready to jump overboard, for fear to be car'd up Channel. I said to him, ' Have a little patience, we shall have a boat in little time now.' He turned unto me in a very sulky manner, and said, ' Who is like you, you are allwayse at home, you don't care where you are car'd.' I smiled, said nothing, but rejoiced within, and said to myself, ' You are saying the truth.' And I thought if it was the will of the Lord that I should be car'd to Copenhagen, that good is the will of the Lord. So in the course of a few minits after saw a boate coming, and so all was well again. I have thought since them days, I mean, since the day that my soul was sanctified, that there did harley one thought pass through me unperseeved in all my waking moments when I was in company talking aboute the things of the world, or the things of God, when in private by myself, or acting of business, my *spirit*, as it were, was in a continual blaze of inward prayer. Well, then, I staid that night at Falmouth, the next morning went to Penryn with my dear little Bettsey in my hand, to see Mr. M——h and his loving family, who was then at Mrs. Scot. The next morning, on Sunday, took a horse and arived at Breage Church town[1] aboute eleven o'clock, where I meet my dear brother Frank, then in his way to Church. As I first took him in surprise, at first I could harley make him sensable I was his brother, being nearley two years without hearing whether I was dead or alife. But when he come to himself as it were, we rejoiced together with exceeding great joy indeed. We went to his house in Rinsey, and after dinner went to see brother John.[2] We sent him word before I was coming.

[1] In West Cornwall every collection of houses is called a town. The village in which the parish church stands is called 'Church town.'
[2] He lived at Prussia Cove.

But he could harley believe it, with the voice of, 'How
can these things be?' But *first* looking out with his
glass saw me yet a *great* way off. Ran to meet me,
fell upon my neck, and said in language like this,
'This is my brother that was dead, but is alive again;
he was loste, but is found.' We passed the afternoon
with him, and in the evning went to Keneggy to see
brother Charles, wh*ere we* meet with many tears of
joy, *and afterwards* returned again to Rinsey in *the
evening*, where we had all our conversation *about*
Hevenly things, *which* was a treat indeed, *after being*
so long *silent* on the subject.

PRINTED BY
SPOTTISWOODE AND CO., NEW-STREET SQUARE
LONDON